A PERSONAL GROWTH GUIDE
FOR YOU TO USE AND GROW

DEVELOPING COURAGE

Understanding confidence for personal improvement and long-term growth

By Claire & Ralph Moody

Your Free Book Is Waiting

Many people struggle with low confidence and low self-esteem, which affects their professional and personal lives. Your thoughts and feelings have a significant impact and this is where issues can manifest. If we don't do something about it, a lack of confidence will hold you back. This book will give you an opportunity to think about your confidence in a different way.

Get your free copy:

www.jcrm.shop

training associates

The authors also own Target Training and the company is recognised as a 5 Star provider by Trustpilot and our testimonials are legendary.

We offer training and coaching services and specialise in Coaching, Training, Management and Personal Development and all our courses can be delivered remotely online.

A sample of our courses include:

- Managing Staff Remotely
- Positive Mental Attitude P.M.A.
- Self-Esteem
- Train the Trainer
- Confidence
- Coaching Skills
- Management Skills
- Leadership Skills
- Mental Health First Aid
- Interview Preparation

Contact us at info@targettrg.co.uk

Our customers love us!

www.targettrg.co.uk or www.targettrg.com

www.targettrg.co.uk
www.jcrmjournals.com

Published in 2020 by JCRM Journals, UK

Designed and Produced by Ralph & Claire Moody

ISBN: 979-8667037316

Effective Leader Journal : A Journal To Build Your Leadership Skills With Power Of Reflection

Available from Amazon and other leading retail outlets.

If you would like us to create a bespoke journal for your organisation or work role contact us on +44 0800 302 9344.

If you enjoyed this journal please leave us a review on Amazon. Thank you.

www.jcrmjournals.com

Retail enquiries to:
info@targettrg.co.uk

Effective
Leadership
Journal

A Journal To Build Your Leadership Skills With Power Of Reflection

RALPH & CLAIRE MOODY

JCRM Journals

target training associates

www.targettrg.co.uk
www.jcrmjournals.com

In case of loss please return to:

....

....

....

www.targettrg.co.uk
www.jcrmjournals.com

EFFECTIVE LEADER JOURNAL

A JOURNAL TO BUILD YOUR LEADERSHIP SKILLS WITH POWER OF REFLECTION

A journal for you to use and grow

Our journals are designed to help individuals in any specific area they would like to change in their lives, both professionally and personally. We use coaching questions to guide your thinking in a different way.

A journal is perfect to write your reflections every day. All you need to do is write for five minutes at the beginning, or end of every day. Writing in a journal can create significant changes in your life when done correctly. We have both benefitted when writing a journal as do millions of others. It's an excellent opportunity to create a habit and build this into your life, make it part of your daily routine.

The purpose of this journal is to encourage you to take control of your leadership skills, it's an opportunity to really understand yourself to achieve your goals and success. Our journals are different, they look at your thinking around the moments of decision making. It is getting to the route of the problem that creates the change looking past the specifics. We have written specific questions for you to use as a guide; these will help you in particular areas. If you sit with just thinking you will not notice as much as if you write. We felt a 100-day journal to begin with where you put all your reflections together would keep things simple for you. If you force yourself to write every day with your thoughts, you will grow in so many ways. You will be so much more successful in your life, if you do this properly. Our aim with this journal is to encourage you to grow and focus to create change. A journal is perfect to record this; keeping all your thoughts and feelings in one place, incredibly powerful and very special.

Try not to make it a tick box exercise, so it becomes a chore. Make it something you look forward to doing, writing your thoughts and feelings on paper so you can reflect and look back. Create the habit and then watch how you develop and grow. The journal includes a page for every day for you to make notes, then separate reflection sheets for every 10 days and then the final page. Reflection is so critical when writing your journal to see what words keep jumping out.

If you find yourself writing the same things recognise this, then think why am I doing this, what change would I like? Then you can reflect on this and what you can do differently. This will help you think in different ways and what you would like to be different, giving you a focus.

Think about how you think and feel, you want to notice differences in yourself to create change, change will be happening if you pay attention.

Forcing yourself to write in a journal will create much more awareness about how you can develop yourself, your mindset and your patterns. There is no doubt you will find yourself growing in confidence and becoming more positive as a leader. It is little changes that move you to create bigger changes, you have to be committed though.

Writing a journal is an amazing journey, good luck and enjoy the very special thoughts and moments as you notice your leadership skills changing.

Ralph & Claire

Ralph & Claire Moody
Founders of JCRM Journals

HOW TO USE THE JOURNAL

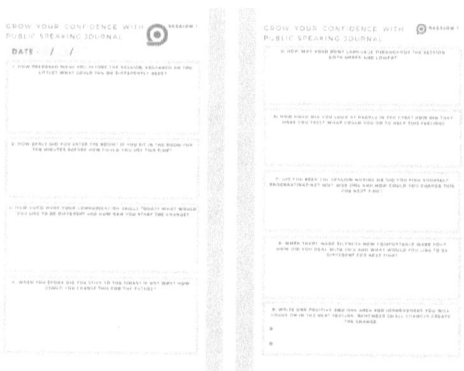

The session sheets are for you to complete each day. Make sure you complete all questions.

Every 10 days complete a review of your actions and reflect on what you have achieved. There is space on the right side for you to make notes along with some wise words and the odd activity.

"Leaders can end up in leadership roles because they are good at their job, not because they are good leaders."

RALPH MOODY

Before we start the journal some pre questions:

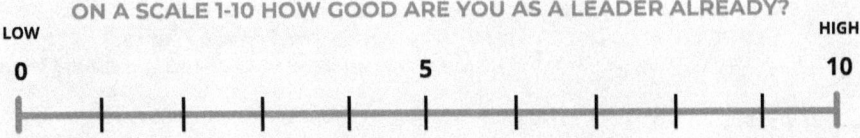

ON A SCALE 1-10 HOW GOOD ARE YOU AS A LEADER ALREADY?

LOW   HIGH

0   5   10

DRAW WHAT LEADERSHIP LOOKS LIKE TO YOU. THEN UNDERNEATH
THINK ABOUT SOME CHANGES YOU WOULD LIKE TO HAVE STARTED BY
THE END OF THE JOURNAL.

DATE:-   /   /

1: HOW WAS YOUR DECISION MAKING TODAY, WHY WAS THIS? WHAT CHANGE COULD YOU MAKE TO MOVE FORWARD INTO TOMORROW?

2: WRITE ONE PROBLEM YOU SOLVED TODAY? HOW DID YOU DEAL WITH THIS? WHAT COULD YOU DO DIFFERENTLY TO IMPROVE?

3: HOW MUCH EMPATHY HAVE YOU SHOWN TODAY, WHY WAS THIS? HOW DID YOU FEEL DEALING WITH EMPATHY? THINK ABOUT A CHANGE TO GROW IN THIS AREA.

4: HOW WAS YOUR PATIENCE TODAY, WHY WAS THIS? WHAT COULD YOU DO DIFFERENTLY TOMORROW?

5: DID YOU DO ANY MENTORING TODAY, WHY WAS THIS? HOW COULD YOU DEVELOP THIS AREA?

6: HOW MUCH ACTIVE LISTENING DID YOU DO TODAY? DID YOU ACTUALLY LISTEN TO UNDERSTAND OR LISTEN TO REPLY? HOW COULD YOU IMPROVE ON THIS AREA FOR TOMORROW?

7: HOW WERE YOUR COMMUNICATION SKILLS TODAY? HOW COULD YOU IMPROVE IN THIS AREA? LITTLE CHANGES TO REALLY UNDERSTAND THE HUGE AREA OF COMMUNICATION WITH DIFFERENT PERSONALITIES.

8: HOW DEPENDABLE DO YOU THINK YOU WERE TODAY? WHY WAS THIS?

9: DID YOU FIND YOURSELF PROCRASTINATING TODAY? HOW COULD YOU CHANGE THIS INTO ACTION?

DATE:-   /   /

1: HOW WAS YOUR DECISION MAKING TODAY, WHY WAS THIS? WHAT CHANGE COULD YOU MAKE TO MOVE FORWARD INTO TOMORROW?

2: WRITE ONE PROBLEM YOU SOLVED TODAY? HOW DID YOU DEAL WITH THIS? WHAT COULD YOU DO DIFFERENTLY TO IMPROVE?

3: HOW MUCH EMPATHY HAVE YOU SHOWN TODAY, WHY WAS THIS? HOW DID YOU FEEL DEALING WITH EMPATHY? THINK ABOUT A CHANGE TO GROW IN THIS AREA.

4: HOW WAS YOUR PATIENCE TODAY, WHY WAS THIS? WHAT COULD YOU DO DIFFERENTLY TOMORROW?

5: DID YOU DO ANY MENTORING TODAY, WHY WAS THIS? HOW COULD YOU DEVELOP THIS AREA?

6: HOW MUCH ACTIVE LISTENING DID YOU DO TODAY? DID YOU ACTUALLY LISTEN TO UNDERSTAND OR LISTEN TO REPLY? HOW COULD YOU IMPROVE ON THIS AREA FOR TOMORROW?

7: HOW WERE YOUR COMMUNICATION SKILLS TODAY? HOW COULD YOU IMPROVE IN THIS AREA? LITTLE CHANGES TO REALLY UNDERSTAND THE HUGE AREA OF COMMUNICATION WITH DIFFERENT PERSONALITIES.

8: HOW DEPENDABLE DO YOU THINK YOU WERE TODAY? WHY WAS THIS?

9: DID YOU FIND YOURSELF PROCRASTINATING TODAY? HOW COULD YOU CHANGE THIS INTO ACTION?

DATE:-   /   /

1: HOW WAS YOUR DECISION MAKING TODAY, WHY WAS THIS?
WHAT CHANGE COULD YOU MAKE TO MOVE FORWARD INTO TOMORROW?

2: WRITE ONE PROBLEM YOU SOLVED TODAY? HOW DID YOU DEAL
WITH THIS? WHAT COULD YOU DO DIFFERENTLY TO IMPROVE?

3: HOW MUCH EMPATHY HAVE YOU SHOWN TODAY, WHY WAS THIS?
HOW DID YOU FEEL DEALING WITH EMPATHY? THINK ABOUT A CHANGE
TO GROW IN THIS AREA.

4: HOW WAS YOUR PATIENCE TODAY, WHY WAS THIS? WHAT
COULD YOU DO DIFFERENTLY TOMORROW?

5: DID YOU DO ANY MENTORING TODAY, WHY WAS THIS? HOW
COULD YOU DEVELOP THIS AREA?

6: HOW MUCH ACTIVE LISTENING DID YOU DO TODAY? DID YOU ACTUALLY LISTEN TO UNDERSTAND OR LISTEN TO REPLY? HOW COULD YOU IMPROVE ON THIS AREA FOR TOMORROW?

7: HOW WERE YOUR COMMUNICATION SKILLS TODAY? HOW COULD YOU IMPROVE IN THIS AREA? LITTLE CHANGES TO REALLY UNDERSTAND THE HUGE AREA OF COMMUNICATION WITH DIFFERENT PERSONALITIES.

8: HOW DEPENDABLE DO YOU THINK YOU WERE TODAY? WHY WAS THIS?

9: DID YOU FIND YOURSELF PROCRASTINATING TODAY? HOW COULD YOU CHANGE THIS INTO ACTION?

DATE:- / /

1: HOW WAS YOUR DECISION MAKING TODAY, WHY WAS THIS? WHAT CHANGE COULD YOU MAKE TO MOVE FORWARD INTO TOMORROW?

2: WRITE ONE PROBLEM YOU SOLVED TODAY? HOW DID YOU DEAL WITH THIS? WHAT COULD YOU DO DIFFERENTLY TO IMPROVE?

3: HOW MUCH EMPATHY HAVE YOU SHOWN TODAY, WHY WAS THIS? HOW DID YOU FEEL DEALING WITH EMPATHY? THINK ABOUT A CHANGE TO GROW IN THIS AREA.

4: HOW WAS YOUR PATIENCE TODAY, WHY WAS THIS? WHAT COULD YOU DO DIFFERENTLY TOMORROW?

5: DID YOU DO ANY MENTORING TODAY, WHY WAS THIS? HOW COULD YOU DEVELOP THIS AREA?

6: HOW MUCH ACTIVE LISTENING DID YOU DO TODAY? DID YOU ACTUALLY LISTEN TO UNDERSTAND OR LISTEN TO REPLY? HOW COULD YOU IMPROVE ON THIS AREA FOR TOMORROW?

7: HOW WERE YOUR COMMUNICATION SKILLS TODAY? HOW COULD YOU IMPROVE IN THIS AREA? LITTLE CHANGES TO REALLY UNDERSTAND THE HUGE AREA OF COMMUNICATION WITH DIFFERENT PERSONALITIES.

8: HOW DEPENDABLE DO YOU THINK YOU WERE TODAY? WHY WAS THIS?

9: DID YOU FIND YOURSELF PROCRASTINATING TODAY? HOW COULD YOU CHANGE THIS INTO ACTION?

DATE:-   /   /

1: HOW WAS YOUR DECISION MAKING TODAY, WHY WAS THIS?
WHAT CHANGE COULD YOU MAKE TO MOVE FORWARD INTO TOMORROW?

2: WRITE ONE PROBLEM YOU SOLVED TODAY? HOW DID YOU DEAL
WITH THIS? WHAT COULD YOU DO DIFFERENTLY TO IMPROVE?

3: HOW MUCH EMPATHY HAVE YOU SHOWN TODAY, WHY WAS THIS?
HOW DID YOU FEEL DEALING WITH EMPATHY? THINK ABOUT A CHANGE
TO GROW IN THIS AREA.

4: HOW WAS YOUR PATIENCE TODAY, WHY WAS THIS? WHAT
COULD YOU DO DIFFERENTLY TOMORROW?

5: DID YOU DO ANY MENTORING TODAY, WHY WAS THIS? HOW
COULD YOU DEVELOP THIS AREA?

6: HOW MUCH ACTIVE LISTENING DID YOU DO TODAY? DID YOU ACTUALLY LISTEN TO UNDERSTAND OR LISTEN TO REPLY? HOW COULD YOU IMPROVE ON THIS AREA FOR TOMORROW?

7: HOW WERE YOUR COMMUNICATION SKILLS TODAY? HOW COULD YOU IMPROVE IN THIS AREA? LITTLE CHANGES TO REALLY UNDERSTAND THE HUGE AREA OF COMMUNICATION WITH DIFFERENT PERSONALITIES.

8: HOW DEPENDABLE DO YOU THINK YOU WERE TODAY? WHY WAS THIS?

9: DID YOU FIND YOURSELF PROCRASTINATING TODAY? HOW COULD YOU CHANGE THIS INTO ACTION?

DATE:-   /   /

1: HOW WAS YOUR DECISION MAKING TODAY, WHY WAS THIS?
WHAT CHANGE COULD YOU MAKE TO MOVE FORWARD INTO TOMORROW?

2: WRITE ONE PROBLEM YOU SOLVED TODAY? HOW DID YOU DEAL
WITH THIS? WHAT COULD YOU DO DIFFERENTLY TO IMPROVE?

3: HOW MUCH EMPATHY HAVE YOU SHOWN TODAY, WHY WAS THIS?
HOW DID YOU FEEL DEALING WITH EMPATHY? THINK ABOUT A CHANGE
TO GROW IN THIS AREA.

4: HOW WAS YOUR PATIENCE TODAY, WHY WAS THIS? WHAT
COULD YOU DO DIFFERENTLY TOMORROW?

5: DID YOU DO ANY MENTORING TODAY, WHY WAS THIS? HOW
COULD YOU DEVELOP THIS AREA?

6: HOW MUCH ACTIVE LISTENING DID YOU DO TODAY? DID YOU ACTUALLY LISTEN TO UNDERSTAND OR LISTEN TO REPLY? HOW COULD YOU IMPROVE ON THIS AREA FOR TOMORROW?

7: HOW WERE YOUR COMMUNICATION SKILLS TODAY? HOW COULD YOU IMPROVE IN THIS AREA? LITTLE CHANGES TO REALLY UNDERSTAND THE HUGE AREA OF COMMUNICATION WITH DIFFERENT PERSONALITIES.

8: HOW DEPENDABLE DO YOU THINK YOU WERE TODAY? WHY WAS THIS?

9: DID YOU FIND YOURSELF PROCRASTINATING TODAY? HOW COULD YOU CHANGE THIS INTO ACTION?

EFFECTIVE LEADER JOURNAL

DATE:-   /   /

1: HOW WAS YOUR DECISION MAKING TODAY, WHY WAS THIS?
WHAT CHANGE COULD YOU MAKE TO MOVE FORWARD INTO TOMORROW?

2: WRITE ONE PROBLEM YOU SOLVED TODAY? HOW DID YOU DEAL
WITH THIS? WHAT COULD YOU DO DIFFERENTLY TO IMPROVE?

3: HOW MUCH EMPATHY HAVE YOU SHOWN TODAY, WHY WAS THIS?
HOW DID YOU FEEL DEALING WITH EMPATHY? THINK ABOUT A CHANGE
TO GROW IN THIS AREA.

4: HOW WAS YOUR PATIENCE TODAY, WHY WAS THIS? WHAT
COULD YOU DO DIFFERENTLY TOMORROW?

5: DID YOU DO ANY MENTORING TODAY, WHY WAS THIS? HOW
COULD YOU DEVELOP THIS AREA?

6: HOW MUCH ACTIVE LISTENING DID YOU DO TODAY? DID YOU ACTUALLY LISTEN TO UNDERSTAND OR LISTEN TO REPLY? HOW COULD YOU IMPROVE ON THIS AREA FOR TOMORROW?

7: HOW WERE YOUR COMMUNICATION SKILLS TODAY? HOW COULD YOU IMPROVE IN THIS AREA? LITTLE CHANGES TO REALLY UNDERSTAND THE HUGE AREA OF COMMUNICATION WITH DIFFERENT PERSONALITIES.

8: HOW DEPENDABLE DO YOU THINK YOU WERE TODAY? WHY WAS THIS?

9: DID YOU FIND YOURSELF PROCRASTINATING TODAY? HOW COULD YOU CHANGE THIS INTO ACTION?

DATE:-   /   /

1: HOW WAS YOUR DECISION MAKING TODAY, WHY WAS THIS? WHAT CHANGE COULD YOU MAKE TO MOVE FORWARD INTO TOMORROW?

2: WRITE ONE PROBLEM YOU SOLVED TODAY? HOW DID YOU DEAL WITH THIS? WHAT COULD YOU DO DIFFERENTLY TO IMPROVE?

3: HOW MUCH EMPATHY HAVE YOU SHOWN TODAY, WHY WAS THIS? HOW DID YOU FEEL DEALING WITH EMPATHY? THINK ABOUT A CHANGE TO GROW IN THIS AREA.

4: HOW WAS YOUR PATIENCE TODAY, WHY WAS THIS? WHAT COULD YOU DO DIFFERENTLY TOMORROW?

5: DID YOU DO ANY MENTORING TODAY, WHY WAS THIS? HOW COULD YOU DEVELOP THIS AREA?

6: HOW MUCH ACTIVE LISTENING DID YOU DO TODAY? DID YOU ACTUALLY LISTEN TO UNDERSTAND OR LISTEN TO REPLY? HOW COULD YOU IMPROVE ON THIS AREA FOR TOMORROW?

7: HOW WERE YOUR COMMUNICATION SKILLS TODAY? HOW COULD YOU IMPROVE IN THIS AREA? LITTLE CHANGES TO REALLY UNDERSTAND THE HUGE AREA OF COMMUNICATION WITH DIFFERENT PERSONALITIES.

8: HOW DEPENDABLE DO YOU THINK YOU WERE TODAY? WHY WAS THIS?

9: DID YOU FIND YOURSELF PROCRASTINATING TODAY? HOW COULD YOU CHANGE THIS INTO ACTION?

EFFECTIVE LEADER JOURNAL

DAY 9

DATE:-   /   /

1: HOW WAS YOUR DECISION MAKING TODAY, WHY WAS THIS? WHAT CHANGE COULD YOU MAKE TO MOVE FORWARD INTO TOMORROW?

2: WRITE ONE PROBLEM YOU SOLVED TODAY? HOW DID YOU DEAL WITH THIS? WHAT COULD YOU DO DIFFERENTLY TO IMPROVE?

3: HOW MUCH EMPATHY HAVE YOU SHOWN TODAY, WHY WAS THIS? HOW DID YOU FEEL DEALING WITH EMPATHY? THINK ABOUT A CHANGE TO GROW IN THIS AREA.

4: HOW WAS YOUR PATIENCE TODAY, WHY WAS THIS? WHAT COULD YOU DO DIFFERENTLY TOMORROW?

5: DID YOU DO ANY MENTORING TODAY, WHY WAS THIS? HOW COULD YOU DEVELOP THIS AREA?

6: HOW MUCH ACTIVE LISTENING DID YOU DO TODAY? DID YOU ACTUALLY LISTEN TO UNDERSTAND OR LISTEN TO REPLY? HOW COULD YOU IMPROVE ON THIS AREA FOR TOMORROW?

7: HOW WERE YOUR COMMUNICATION SKILLS TODAY? HOW COULD YOU IMPROVE IN THIS AREA? LITTLE CHANGES TO REALLY UNDERSTAND THE HUGE AREA OF COMMUNICATION WITH DIFFERENT PERSONALITIES.

8: HOW DEPENDABLE DO YOU THINK YOU WERE TODAY? WHY WAS THIS?

9: DID YOU FIND YOURSELF PROCRASTINATING TODAY? HOW COULD YOU CHANGE THIS INTO ACTION?

DATE:-   /   /

1: HOW WAS YOUR DECISION MAKING TODAY, WHY WAS THIS?
WHAT CHANGE COULD YOU MAKE TO MOVE FORWARD INTO TOMORROW?

2: WRITE ONE PROBLEM YOU SOLVED TODAY? HOW DID YOU DEAL
WITH THIS? WHAT COULD YOU DO DIFFERENTLY TO IMPROVE?

3: HOW MUCH EMPATHY HAVE YOU SHOWN TODAY, WHY WAS THIS?
HOW DID YOU FEEL DEALING WITH EMPATHY? THINK ABOUT A CHANGE
TO GROW IN THIS AREA.

4: HOW WAS YOUR PATIENCE TODAY, WHY WAS THIS? WHAT
COULD YOU DO DIFFERENTLY TOMORROW?

5: DID YOU DO ANY MENTORING TODAY, WHY WAS THIS? HOW
COULD YOU DEVELOP THIS AREA?

6: HOW MUCH ACTIVE LISTENING DID YOU DO TODAY? DID YOU ACTUALLY LISTEN TO UNDERSTAND OR LISTEN TO REPLY? HOW COULD YOU IMPROVE ON THIS AREA FOR TOMORROW?

7: HOW WERE YOUR COMMUNICATION SKILLS TODAY? HOW COULD YOU IMPROVE IN THIS AREA? LITTLE CHANGES TO REALLY UNDERSTAND THE HUGE AREA OF COMMUNICATION WITH DIFFERENT PERSONALITIES.

8: HOW DEPENDABLE DO YOU THINK YOU WERE TODAY? WHY WAS THIS?

9: DID YOU FIND YOURSELF PROCRASTINATING TODAY? HOW COULD YOU CHANGE THIS INTO ACTION?

1: HOW HAVE I GROWN OVER THE LAST 10 DAYS

2: WHAT AM I GOING TO FOCUS ON OVER THE NEXT 10 DAYS?

3: WHAT FIVE THINGS AM I POSITIVELY TAKING FROM THE LAST 10 DAYS AND MOVING THEM FORWARD INTO THE NEXT 10 DAYS.

-
-
-
-
-

4: WHAT KEY AREAS WOULD I LIKE TO CONCENTRATE ON?

"Leaders can end up in leadership roles because they are good at their job, not because they are good leaders."

RALPH MOODY

DATE:-   /   /

1: HOW WAS YOUR DECISION MAKING TODAY, WHY WAS THIS? WHAT CHANGE COULD YOU MAKE TO MOVE FORWARD INTO TOMORROW?

2: WRITE ONE PROBLEM YOU SOLVED TODAY? HOW DID YOU DEAL WITH THIS? WHAT COULD YOU DO DIFFERENTLY TO IMPROVE?

3: HOW MUCH EMPATHY HAVE YOU SHOWN TODAY, WHY WAS THIS? HOW DID YOU FEEL DEALING WITH EMPATHY? THINK ABOUT A CHANGE TO GROW IN THIS AREA.

4: HOW WAS YOUR PATIENCE TODAY, WHY WAS THIS? WHAT COULD YOU DO DIFFERENTLY TOMORROW?

5: DID YOU DO ANY MENTORING TODAY, WHY WAS THIS? HOW COULD YOU DEVELOP THIS AREA?

6: HOW MUCH ACTIVE LISTENING DID YOU DO TODAY? DID YOU ACTUALLY LISTEN TO UNDERSTAND OR LISTEN TO REPLY? HOW COULD YOU IMPROVE ON THIS AREA FOR TOMORROW?

7: HOW WERE YOUR COMMUNICATION SKILLS TODAY? HOW COULD YOU IMPROVE IN THIS AREA? LITTLE CHANGES TO REALLY UNDERSTAND THE HUGE AREA OF COMMUNICATION WITH DIFFERENT PERSONALITIES.

8: HOW DEPENDABLE DO YOU THINK YOU WERE TODAY? WHY WAS THIS?

9: DID YOU FIND YOURSELF PROCRASTINATING TODAY? HOW COULD YOU CHANGE THIS INTO ACTION?

DATE:-   /   /

1: HOW WAS YOUR DECISION MAKING TODAY, WHY WAS THIS? WHAT CHANGE COULD YOU MAKE TO MOVE FORWARD INTO TOMORROW?

2: WRITE ONE PROBLEM YOU SOLVED TODAY? HOW DID YOU DEAL WITH THIS? WHAT COULD YOU DO DIFFERENTLY TO IMPROVE?

3: HOW MUCH EMPATHY HAVE YOU SHOWN TODAY, WHY WAS THIS? HOW DID YOU FEEL DEALING WITH EMPATHY? THINK ABOUT A CHANGE TO GROW IN THIS AREA.

4: HOW WAS YOUR PATIENCE TODAY, WHY WAS THIS? WHAT COULD YOU DO DIFFERENTLY TOMORROW?

5: DID YOU DO ANY MENTORING TODAY, WHY WAS THIS? HOW COULD YOU DEVELOP THIS AREA?

6: HOW MUCH ACTIVE LISTENING DID YOU DO TODAY? DID YOU ACTUALLY LISTEN TO UNDERSTAND OR LISTEN TO REPLY? HOW COULD YOU IMPROVE ON THIS AREA FOR TOMORROW?

7: HOW WERE YOUR COMMUNICATION SKILLS TODAY? HOW COULD YOU IMPROVE IN THIS AREA? LITTLE CHANGES TO REALLY UNDERSTAND THE HUGE AREA OF COMMUNICATION WITH DIFFERENT PERSONALITIES.

8: HOW DEPENDABLE DO YOU THINK YOU WERE TODAY? WHY WAS THIS?

9: DID YOU FIND YOURSELF PROCRASTINATING TODAY? HOW COULD YOU CHANGE THIS INTO ACTION?

DATE:-   /   /

1: HOW WAS YOUR DECISION MAKING TODAY, WHY WAS THIS?
WHAT CHANGE COULD YOU MAKE TO MOVE FORWARD INTO TOMORROW?

2: WRITE ONE PROBLEM YOU SOLVED TODAY? HOW DID YOU DEAL
WITH THIS? WHAT COULD YOU DO DIFFERENTLY TO IMPROVE?

3: HOW MUCH EMPATHY HAVE YOU SHOWN TODAY, WHY WAS THIS?
HOW DID YOU FEEL DEALING WITH EMPATHY? THINK ABOUT A CHANGE
TO GROW IN THIS AREA.

4: HOW WAS YOUR PATIENCE TODAY, WHY WAS THIS? WHAT
COULD YOU DO DIFFERENTLY TOMORROW?

5: DID YOU DO ANY MENTORING TODAY, WHY WAS THIS? HOW
COULD YOU DEVELOP THIS AREA?

6: HOW MUCH ACTIVE LISTENING DID YOU DO TODAY? DID YOU ACTUALLY LISTEN TO UNDERSTAND OR LISTEN TO REPLY? HOW COULD YOU IMPROVE ON THIS AREA FOR TOMORROW?

7: HOW WERE YOUR COMMUNICATION SKILLS TODAY? HOW COULD YOU IMPROVE IN THIS AREA? LITTLE CHANGES TO REALLY UNDERSTAND THE HUGE AREA OF COMMUNICATION WITH DIFFERENT PERSONALITIES.

8: HOW DEPENDABLE DO YOU THINK YOU WERE TODAY? WHY WAS THIS?

9: DID YOU FIND YOURSELF PROCRASTINATING TODAY? HOW COULD YOU CHANGE THIS INTO ACTION?

DATE:-   /   /

1: HOW WAS YOUR DECISION MAKING TODAY, WHY WAS THIS? WHAT CHANGE COULD YOU MAKE TO MOVE FORWARD INTO TOMORROW?

2: WRITE ONE PROBLEM YOU SOLVED TODAY? HOW DID YOU DEAL WITH THIS? WHAT COULD YOU DO DIFFERENTLY TO IMPROVE?

3: HOW MUCH EMPATHY HAVE YOU SHOWN TODAY, WHY WAS THIS? HOW DID YOU FEEL DEALING WITH EMPATHY? THINK ABOUT A CHANGE TO GROW IN THIS AREA.

4: HOW WAS YOUR PATIENCE TODAY, WHY WAS THIS? WHAT COULD YOU DO DIFFERENTLY TOMORROW?

5: DID YOU DO ANY MENTORING TODAY, WHY WAS THIS? HOW COULD YOU DEVELOP THIS AREA?

6: HOW MUCH ACTIVE LISTENING DID YOU DO TODAY? DID YOU ACTUALLY LISTEN TO UNDERSTAND OR LISTEN TO REPLY? HOW COULD YOU IMPROVE ON THIS AREA FOR TOMORROW?

7: HOW WERE YOUR COMMUNICATION SKILLS TODAY? HOW COULD YOU IMPROVE IN THIS AREA? LITTLE CHANGES TO REALLY UNDERSTAND THE HUGE AREA OF COMMUNICATION WITH DIFFERENT PERSONALITIES.

8: HOW DEPENDABLE DO YOU THINK YOU WERE TODAY? WHY WAS THIS?

9: DID YOU FIND YOURSELF PROCRASTINATING TODAY? HOW COULD YOU CHANGE THIS INTO ACTION?

DATE:-   /   /

1: HOW WAS YOUR DECISION MAKING TODAY, WHY WAS THIS? WHAT CHANGE COULD YOU MAKE TO MOVE FORWARD INTO TOMORROW?

2: WRITE ONE PROBLEM YOU SOLVED TODAY? HOW DID YOU DEAL WITH THIS? WHAT COULD YOU DO DIFFERENTLY TO IMPROVE?

3: HOW MUCH EMPATHY HAVE YOU SHOWN TODAY, WHY WAS THIS? HOW DID YOU FEEL DEALING WITH EMPATHY? THINK ABOUT A CHANGE TO GROW IN THIS AREA.

4: HOW WAS YOUR PATIENCE TODAY, WHY WAS THIS? WHAT COULD YOU DO DIFFERENTLY TOMORROW?

5: DID YOU DO ANY MENTORING TODAY, WHY WAS THIS? HOW COULD YOU DEVELOP THIS AREA?

6: HOW MUCH ACTIVE LISTENING DID YOU DO TODAY? DID YOU ACTUALLY LISTEN TO UNDERSTAND OR LISTEN TO REPLY? HOW COULD YOU IMPROVE ON THIS AREA FOR TOMORROW?

7: HOW WERE YOUR COMMUNICATION SKILLS TODAY? HOW COULD YOU IMPROVE IN THIS AREA? LITTLE CHANGES TO REALLY UNDERSTAND THE HUGE AREA OF COMMUNICATION WITH DIFFERENT PERSONALITIES.

8: HOW DEPENDABLE DO YOU THINK YOU WERE TODAY? WHY WAS THIS?

9: DID YOU FIND YOURSELF PROCRASTINATING TODAY? HOW COULD YOU CHANGE THIS INTO ACTION?

DATE:-   /   /

1: HOW WAS YOUR DECISION MAKING TODAY, WHY WAS THIS?
WHAT CHANGE COULD YOU MAKE TO MOVE FORWARD INTO TOMORROW?

2: WRITE ONE PROBLEM YOU SOLVED TODAY? HOW DID YOU DEAL
WITH THIS? WHAT COULD YOU DO DIFFERENTLY TO IMPROVE?

3: HOW MUCH EMPATHY HAVE YOU SHOWN TODAY, WHY WAS THIS?
HOW DID YOU FEEL DEALING WITH EMPATHY? THINK ABOUT A CHANGE
TO GROW IN THIS AREA.

4: HOW WAS YOUR PATIENCE TODAY, WHY WAS THIS? WHAT
COULD YOU DO DIFFERENTLY TOMORROW?

5: DID YOU DO ANY MENTORING TODAY, WHY WAS THIS? HOW
COULD YOU DEVELOP THIS AREA?

6: HOW MUCH ACTIVE LISTENING DID YOU DO TODAY? DID YOU ACTUALLY LISTEN TO UNDERSTAND OR LISTEN TO REPLY? HOW COULD YOU IMPROVE ON THIS AREA FOR TOMORROW?

7: HOW WERE YOUR COMMUNICATION SKILLS TODAY? HOW COULD YOU IMPROVE IN THIS AREA? LITTLE CHANGES TO REALLY UNDERSTAND THE HUGE AREA OF COMMUNICATION WITH DIFFERENT PERSONALITIES.

8: HOW DEPENDABLE DO YOU THINK YOU WERE TODAY? WHY WAS THIS?

9: DID YOU FIND YOURSELF PROCRASTINATING TODAY? HOW COULD YOU CHANGE THIS INTO ACTION?

DATE:-   /   /

1: HOW WAS YOUR DECISION MAKING TODAY, WHY WAS THIS?
WHAT CHANGE COULD YOU MAKE TO MOVE FORWARD INTO TOMORROW?

2: WRITE ONE PROBLEM YOU SOLVED TODAY? HOW DID YOU DEAL
WITH THIS? WHAT COULD YOU DO DIFFERENTLY TO IMPROVE?

3: HOW MUCH EMPATHY HAVE YOU SHOWN TODAY, WHY WAS THIS?
HOW DID YOU FEEL DEALING WITH EMPATHY? THINK ABOUT A CHANGE
TO GROW IN THIS AREA.

4: HOW WAS YOUR PATIENCE TODAY, WHY WAS THIS? WHAT
COULD YOU DO DIFFERENTLY TOMORROW?

5: DID YOU DO ANY MENTORING TODAY, WHY WAS THIS? HOW
COULD YOU DEVELOP THIS AREA?

6: HOW MUCH ACTIVE LISTENING DID YOU DO TODAY? DID YOU ACTUALLY LISTEN TO UNDERSTAND OR LISTEN TO REPLY? HOW COULD YOU IMPROVE ON THIS AREA FOR TOMORROW?

7: HOW WERE YOUR COMMUNICATION SKILLS TODAY? HOW COULD YOU IMPROVE IN THIS AREA? LITTLE CHANGES TO REALLY UNDERSTAND THE HUGE AREA OF COMMUNICATION WITH DIFFERENT PERSONALITIES.

8: HOW DEPENDABLE DO YOU THINK YOU WERE TODAY? WHY WAS THIS?

9: DID YOU FIND YOURSELF PROCRASTINATING TODAY? HOW COULD YOU CHANGE THIS INTO ACTION?

DATE:-   /   /

1: HOW WAS YOUR DECISION MAKING TODAY, WHY WAS THIS? WHAT CHANGE COULD YOU MAKE TO MOVE FORWARD INTO TOMORROW?

2: WRITE ONE PROBLEM YOU SOLVED TODAY? HOW DID YOU DEAL WITH THIS? WHAT COULD YOU DO DIFFERENTLY TO IMPROVE?

3: HOW MUCH EMPATHY HAVE YOU SHOWN TODAY, WHY WAS THIS? HOW DID YOU FEEL DEALING WITH EMPATHY? THINK ABOUT A CHANGE TO GROW IN THIS AREA.

4: HOW WAS YOUR PATIENCE TODAY, WHY WAS THIS? WHAT COULD YOU DO DIFFERENTLY TOMORROW?

5: DID YOU DO ANY MENTORING TODAY, WHY WAS THIS? HOW COULD YOU DEVELOP THIS AREA?

6: HOW MUCH ACTIVE LISTENING DID YOU DO TODAY? DID YOU ACTUALLY LISTEN TO UNDERSTAND OR LISTEN TO REPLY? HOW COULD YOU IMPROVE ON THIS AREA FOR TOMORROW?

7: HOW WERE YOUR COMMUNICATION SKILLS TODAY? HOW COULD YOU IMPROVE IN THIS AREA? LITTLE CHANGES TO REALLY UNDERSTAND THE HUGE AREA OF COMMUNICATION WITH DIFFERENT PERSONALITIES.

8: HOW DEPENDABLE DO YOU THINK YOU WERE TODAY? WHY WAS THIS?

9: DID YOU FIND YOURSELF PROCRASTINATING TODAY? HOW COULD YOU CHANGE THIS INTO ACTION?

DATE:-   /   /

1: HOW WAS YOUR DECISION MAKING TODAY, WHY WAS THIS? WHAT CHANGE COULD YOU MAKE TO MOVE FORWARD INTO TOMORROW?

2: WRITE ONE PROBLEM YOU SOLVED TODAY? HOW DID YOU DEAL WITH THIS? WHAT COULD YOU DO DIFFERENTLY TO IMPROVE?

3: HOW MUCH EMPATHY HAVE YOU SHOWN TODAY, WHY WAS THIS? HOW DID YOU FEEL DEALING WITH EMPATHY? THINK ABOUT A CHANGE TO GROW IN THIS AREA.

4: HOW WAS YOUR PATIENCE TODAY, WHY WAS THIS? WHAT COULD YOU DO DIFFERENTLY TOMORROW?

5: DID YOU DO ANY MENTORING TODAY, WHY WAS THIS? HOW COULD YOU DEVELOP THIS AREA?

6: HOW MUCH ACTIVE LISTENING DID YOU DO TODAY? DID YOU ACTUALLY LISTEN TO UNDERSTAND OR LISTEN TO REPLY? HOW COULD YOU IMPROVE ON THIS AREA FOR TOMORROW?

7: HOW WERE YOUR COMMUNICATION SKILLS TODAY? HOW COULD YOU IMPROVE IN THIS AREA? LITTLE CHANGES TO REALLY UNDERSTAND THE HUGE AREA OF COMMUNICATION WITH DIFFERENT PERSONALITIES.

8: HOW DEPENDABLE DO YOU THINK YOU WERE TODAY? WHY WAS THIS?

9: DID YOU FIND YOURSELF PROCRASTINATING TODAY? HOW COULD YOU CHANGE THIS INTO ACTION?

DATE:-   /   /

1: HOW WAS YOUR DECISION MAKING TODAY, WHY WAS THIS?
WHAT CHANGE COULD YOU MAKE TO MOVE FORWARD INTO TOMORROW?

2: WRITE ONE PROBLEM YOU SOLVED TODAY? HOW DID YOU DEAL
WITH THIS? WHAT COULD YOU DO DIFFERENTLY TO IMPROVE?

3: HOW MUCH EMPATHY HAVE YOU SHOWN TODAY, WHY WAS THIS?
HOW DID YOU FEEL DEALING WITH EMPATHY? THINK ABOUT A CHANGE
TO GROW IN THIS AREA.

4: HOW WAS YOUR PATIENCE TODAY, WHY WAS THIS? WHAT
COULD YOU DO DIFFERENTLY TOMORROW?

5: DID YOU DO ANY MENTORING TODAY, WHY WAS THIS? HOW
COULD YOU DEVELOP THIS AREA?

EFFECTIVE LEADER JOURNAL

6: HOW MUCH ACTIVE LISTENING DID YOU DO TODAY? DID YOU ACTUALLY LISTEN TO UNDERSTAND OR LISTEN TO REPLY? HOW COULD YOU IMPROVE ON THIS AREA FOR TOMORROW?

7: HOW WERE YOUR COMMUNICATION SKILLS TODAY? HOW COULD YOU IMPROVE IN THIS AREA? LITTLE CHANGES TO REALLY UNDERSTAND THE HUGE AREA OF COMMUNICATION WITH DIFFERENT PERSONALITIES.

8: HOW DEPENDABLE DO YOU THINK YOU WERE TODAY? WHY WAS THIS?

9: DID YOU FIND YOURSELF PROCRASTINATING TODAY? HOW COULD YOU CHANGE THIS INTO ACTION?

1: HOW HAVE I GROWN OVER THE LAST 10 DAYS

2: WHAT AM I GOING TO FOCUS ON OVER THE NEXT 10 DAYS?

3: WHAT FIVE THINGS AM I POSITIVELY TAKING FROM THE LAST 10 DAYS AND MOVING THEM FORWARD INTO THE NEXT 10 DAYS.

-
-
-
-
-

4: WHAT KEY AREAS WOULD I LIKE TO CONCENTRATE ON?

"People like to be told what to do, don't dither. Decide and act then accept the consequences. Wrong decisions are better than no decisions."

CLAIRE MOODY

DATE:-   /   /

1: HOW WAS YOUR DECISION MAKING TODAY, WHY WAS THIS?
WHAT CHANGE COULD YOU MAKE TO MOVE FORWARD INTO TOMORROW?

2: WRITE ONE PROBLEM YOU SOLVED TODAY? HOW DID YOU DEAL
WITH THIS? WHAT COULD YOU DO DIFFERENTLY TO IMPROVE?

3: HOW MUCH EMPATHY HAVE YOU SHOWN TODAY, WHY WAS THIS?
HOW DID YOU FEEL DEALING WITH EMPATHY? THINK ABOUT A CHANGE
TO GROW IN THIS AREA.

4: HOW WAS YOUR PATIENCE TODAY, WHY WAS THIS? WHAT
COULD YOU DO DIFFERENTLY TOMORROW?

5: DID YOU DO ANY MENTORING TODAY, WHY WAS THIS? HOW
COULD YOU DEVELOP THIS AREA?

6: HOW MUCH ACTIVE LISTENING DID YOU DO TODAY? DID YOU ACTUALLY LISTEN TO UNDERSTAND OR LISTEN TO REPLY? HOW COULD YOU IMPROVE ON THIS AREA FOR TOMORROW?

7: HOW WERE YOUR COMMUNICATION SKILLS TODAY? HOW COULD YOU IMPROVE IN THIS AREA? LITTLE CHANGES TO REALLY UNDERSTAND THE HUGE AREA OF COMMUNICATION WITH DIFFERENT PERSONALITIES.

8: HOW DEPENDABLE DO YOU THINK YOU WERE TODAY? WHY WAS THIS?

9: DID YOU FIND YOURSELF PROCRASTINATING TODAY? HOW COULD YOU CHANGE THIS INTO ACTION?

DATE:-   /   /

1: HOW WAS YOUR DECISION MAKING TODAY, WHY WAS THIS? WHAT CHANGE COULD YOU MAKE TO MOVE FORWARD INTO TOMORROW?

2: WRITE ONE PROBLEM YOU SOLVED TODAY? HOW DID YOU DEAL WITH THIS? WHAT COULD YOU DO DIFFERENTLY TO IMPROVE?

3: HOW MUCH EMPATHY HAVE YOU SHOWN TODAY, WHY WAS THIS? HOW DID YOU FEEL DEALING WITH EMPATHY? THINK ABOUT A CHANGE TO GROW IN THIS AREA.

4: HOW WAS YOUR PATIENCE TODAY, WHY WAS THIS? WHAT COULD YOU DO DIFFERENTLY TOMORROW?

5: DID YOU DO ANY MENTORING TODAY, WHY WAS THIS? HOW COULD YOU DEVELOP THIS AREA?

6: HOW MUCH ACTIVE LISTENING DID YOU DO TODAY? DID YOU ACTUALLY LISTEN TO UNDERSTAND OR LISTEN TO REPLY? HOW COULD YOU IMPROVE ON THIS AREA FOR TOMORROW?

7: HOW WERE YOUR COMMUNICATION SKILLS TODAY? HOW COULD YOU IMPROVE IN THIS AREA? LITTLE CHANGES TO REALLY UNDERSTAND THE HUGE AREA OF COMMUNICATION WITH DIFFERENT PERSONALITIES.

8: HOW DEPENDABLE DO YOU THINK YOU WERE TODAY? WHY WAS THIS?

9: DID YOU FIND YOURSELF PROCRASTINATING TODAY? HOW COULD YOU CHANGE THIS INTO ACTION?

DATE:-   /   /

1: HOW WAS YOUR DECISION MAKING TODAY, WHY WAS THIS?
WHAT CHANGE COULD YOU MAKE TO MOVE FORWARD INTO TOMORROW?

2: WRITE ONE PROBLEM YOU SOLVED TODAY? HOW DID YOU DEAL
WITH THIS? WHAT COULD YOU DO DIFFERENTLY TO IMPROVE?

3: HOW MUCH EMPATHY HAVE YOU SHOWN TODAY, WHY WAS THIS?
HOW DID YOU FEEL DEALING WITH EMPATHY? THINK ABOUT A CHANGE
TO GROW IN THIS AREA.

4: HOW WAS YOUR PATIENCE TODAY, WHY WAS THIS? WHAT
COULD YOU DO DIFFERENTLY TOMORROW?

5: DID YOU DO ANY MENTORING TODAY, WHY WAS THIS? HOW
COULD YOU DEVELOP THIS AREA?

6: HOW MUCH ACTIVE LISTENING DID YOU DO TODAY? DID YOU ACTUALLY LISTEN TO UNDERSTAND OR LISTEN TO REPLY? HOW COULD YOU IMPROVE ON THIS AREA FOR TOMORROW?

7: HOW WERE YOUR COMMUNICATION SKILLS TODAY? HOW COULD YOU IMPROVE IN THIS AREA? LITTLE CHANGES TO REALLY UNDERSTAND THE HUGE AREA OF COMMUNICATION WITH DIFFERENT PERSONALITIES.

8: HOW DEPENDABLE DO YOU THINK YOU WERE TODAY? WHY WAS THIS?

9: DID YOU FIND YOURSELF PROCRASTINATING TODAY? HOW COULD YOU CHANGE THIS INTO ACTION?

DATE:-   /   /

1: HOW WAS YOUR DECISION MAKING TODAY, WHY WAS THIS?
WHAT CHANGE COULD YOU MAKE TO MOVE FORWARD INTO TOMORROW?

2: WRITE ONE PROBLEM YOU SOLVED TODAY? HOW DID YOU DEAL
WITH THIS? WHAT COULD YOU DO DIFFERENTLY TO IMPROVE?

3: HOW MUCH EMPATHY HAVE YOU SHOWN TODAY, WHY WAS THIS?
HOW DID YOU FEEL DEALING WITH EMPATHY? THINK ABOUT A CHANGE
TO GROW IN THIS AREA.

4: HOW WAS YOUR PATIENCE TODAY, WHY WAS THIS? WHAT
COULD YOU DO DIFFERENTLY TOMORROW?

5: DID YOU DO ANY MENTORING TODAY, WHY WAS THIS? HOW
COULD YOU DEVELOP THIS AREA?

6: HOW MUCH ACTIVE LISTENING DID YOU DO TODAY? DID YOU ACTUALLY LISTEN TO UNDERSTAND OR LISTEN TO REPLY? HOW COULD YOU IMPROVE ON THIS AREA FOR TOMORROW?

7: HOW WERE YOUR COMMUNICATION SKILLS TODAY? HOW COULD YOU IMPROVE IN THIS AREA? LITTLE CHANGES TO REALLY UNDERSTAND THE HUGE AREA OF COMMUNICATION WITH DIFFERENT PERSONALITIES.

8: HOW DEPENDABLE DO YOU THINK YOU WERE TODAY? WHY WAS THIS?

9: DID YOU FIND YOURSELF PROCRASTINATING TODAY? HOW COULD YOU CHANGE THIS INTO ACTION?

DATE:-   /   /

1: HOW WAS YOUR DECISION MAKING TODAY, WHY WAS THIS?
WHAT CHANGE COULD YOU MAKE TO MOVE FORWARD INTO TOMORROW?

2: WRITE ONE PROBLEM YOU SOLVED TODAY? HOW DID YOU DEAL
WITH THIS? WHAT COULD YOU DO DIFFERENTLY TO IMPROVE?

3: HOW MUCH EMPATHY HAVE YOU SHOWN TODAY, WHY WAS THIS?
HOW DID YOU FEEL DEALING WITH EMPATHY? THINK ABOUT A CHANGE
TO GROW IN THIS AREA.

4: HOW WAS YOUR PATIENCE TODAY, WHY WAS THIS? WHAT
COULD YOU DO DIFFERENTLY TOMORROW?

5: DID YOU DO ANY MENTORING TODAY, WHY WAS THIS? HOW
COULD YOU DEVELOP THIS AREA?

6: HOW MUCH ACTIVE LISTENING DID YOU DO TODAY? DID YOU ACTUALLY LISTEN TO UNDERSTAND OR LISTEN TO REPLY? HOW COULD YOU IMPROVE ON THIS AREA FOR TOMORROW?

7: HOW WERE YOUR COMMUNICATION SKILLS TODAY? HOW COULD YOU IMPROVE IN THIS AREA? LITTLE CHANGES TO REALLY UNDERSTAND THE HUGE AREA OF COMMUNICATION WITH DIFFERENT PERSONALITIES.

8: HOW DEPENDABLE DO YOU THINK YOU WERE TODAY? WHY WAS THIS?

9: DID YOU FIND YOURSELF PROCRASTINATING TODAY? HOW COULD YOU CHANGE THIS INTO ACTION?

DATE:-   /   /

1: HOW WAS YOUR DECISION MAKING TODAY, WHY WAS THIS?
WHAT CHANGE COULD YOU MAKE TO MOVE FORWARD INTO TOMORROW?

2: WRITE ONE PROBLEM YOU SOLVED TODAY? HOW DID YOU DEAL
WITH THIS? WHAT COULD YOU DO DIFFERENTLY TO IMPROVE?

3: HOW MUCH EMPATHY HAVE YOU SHOWN TODAY, WHY WAS THIS?
HOW DID YOU FEEL DEALING WITH EMPATHY? THINK ABOUT A CHANGE
TO GROW IN THIS AREA.

4: HOW WAS YOUR PATIENCE TODAY, WHY WAS THIS? WHAT
COULD YOU DO DIFFERENTLY TOMORROW?

5: DID YOU DO ANY MENTORING TODAY, WHY WAS THIS? HOW
COULD YOU DEVELOP THIS AREA?

6: HOW MUCH ACTIVE LISTENING DID YOU DO TODAY? DID YOU ACTUALLY LISTEN TO UNDERSTAND OR LISTEN TO REPLY? HOW COULD YOU IMPROVE ON THIS AREA FOR TOMORROW?

7: HOW WERE YOUR COMMUNICATION SKILLS TODAY? HOW COULD YOU IMPROVE IN THIS AREA? LITTLE CHANGES TO REALLY UNDERSTAND THE HUGE AREA OF COMMUNICATION WITH DIFFERENT PERSONALITIES.

8: HOW DEPENDABLE DO YOU THINK YOU WERE TODAY? WHY WAS THIS?

9: DID YOU FIND YOURSELF PROCRASTINATING TODAY? HOW COULD YOU CHANGE THIS INTO ACTION?

DATE:-   /   /

1: HOW WAS YOUR DECISION MAKING TODAY, WHY WAS THIS?
WHAT CHANGE COULD YOU MAKE TO MOVE FORWARD INTO TOMORROW?

2: WRITE ONE PROBLEM YOU SOLVED TODAY? HOW DID YOU DEAL
WITH THIS? WHAT COULD YOU DO DIFFERENTLY TO IMPROVE?

3: HOW MUCH EMPATHY HAVE YOU SHOWN TODAY, WHY WAS THIS?
HOW DID YOU FEEL DEALING WITH EMPATHY? THINK ABOUT A CHANGE
TO GROW IN THIS AREA.

4: HOW WAS YOUR PATIENCE TODAY, WHY WAS THIS? WHAT
COULD YOU DO DIFFERENTLY TOMORROW?

5: DID YOU DO ANY MENTORING TODAY, WHY WAS THIS? HOW
COULD YOU DEVELOP THIS AREA?

6: HOW MUCH ACTIVE LISTENING DID YOU DO TODAY? DID YOU ACTUALLY LISTEN TO UNDERSTAND OR LISTEN TO REPLY? HOW COULD YOU IMPROVE ON THIS AREA FOR TOMORROW?

7: HOW WERE YOUR COMMUNICATION SKILLS TODAY? HOW COULD YOU IMPROVE IN THIS AREA? LITTLE CHANGES TO REALLY UNDERSTAND THE HUGE AREA OF COMMUNICATION WITH DIFFERENT PERSONALITIES.

8: HOW DEPENDABLE DO YOU THINK YOU WERE TODAY? WHY WAS THIS?

9: DID YOU FIND YOURSELF PROCRASTINATING TODAY? HOW COULD YOU CHANGE THIS INTO ACTION?

DATE:-   /   /

1: HOW WAS YOUR DECISION MAKING TODAY, WHY WAS THIS? WHAT CHANGE COULD YOU MAKE TO MOVE FORWARD INTO TOMORROW?

2: WRITE ONE PROBLEM YOU SOLVED TODAY? HOW DID YOU DEAL WITH THIS? WHAT COULD YOU DO DIFFERENTLY TO IMPROVE?

3: HOW MUCH EMPATHY HAVE YOU SHOWN TODAY, WHY WAS THIS? HOW DID YOU FEEL DEALING WITH EMPATHY? THINK ABOUT A CHANGE TO GROW IN THIS AREA.

4: HOW WAS YOUR PATIENCE TODAY, WHY WAS THIS? WHAT COULD YOU DO DIFFERENTLY TOMORROW?

5: DID YOU DO ANY MENTORING TODAY, WHY WAS THIS? HOW COULD YOU DEVELOP THIS AREA?

6: HOW MUCH ACTIVE LISTENING DID YOU DO TODAY? DID YOU ACTUALLY LISTEN TO UNDERSTAND OR LISTEN TO REPLY? HOW COULD YOU IMPROVE ON THIS AREA FOR TOMORROW?

7: HOW WERE YOUR COMMUNICATION SKILLS TODAY? HOW COULD YOU IMPROVE IN THIS AREA? LITTLE CHANGES TO REALLY UNDERSTAND THE HUGE AREA OF COMMUNICATION WITH DIFFERENT PERSONALITIES.

8: HOW DEPENDABLE DO YOU THINK YOU WERE TODAY? WHY WAS THIS?

9: DID YOU FIND YOURSELF PROCRASTINATING TODAY? HOW COULD YOU CHANGE THIS INTO ACTION?

DATE:-   /   /

1: HOW WAS YOUR DECISION MAKING TODAY, WHY WAS THIS?
WHAT CHANGE COULD YOU MAKE TO MOVE FORWARD INTO TOMORROW?

2: WRITE ONE PROBLEM YOU SOLVED TODAY? HOW DID YOU DEAL
WITH THIS? WHAT COULD YOU DO DIFFERENTLY TO IMPROVE?

3: HOW MUCH EMPATHY HAVE YOU SHOWN TODAY, WHY WAS THIS?
HOW DID YOU FEEL DEALING WITH EMPATHY? THINK ABOUT A CHANGE
TO GROW IN THIS AREA.

4: HOW WAS YOUR PATIENCE TODAY, WHY WAS THIS? WHAT
COULD YOU DO DIFFERENTLY TOMORROW?

5: DID YOU DO ANY MENTORING TODAY, WHY WAS THIS? HOW
COULD YOU DEVELOP THIS AREA?

6: HOW MUCH ACTIVE LISTENING DID YOU DO TODAY? DID YOU ACTUALLY LISTEN TO UNDERSTAND OR LISTEN TO REPLY? HOW COULD YOU IMPROVE ON THIS AREA FOR TOMORROW?

7: HOW WERE YOUR COMMUNICATION SKILLS TODAY? HOW COULD YOU IMPROVE IN THIS AREA? LITTLE CHANGES TO REALLY UNDERSTAND THE HUGE AREA OF COMMUNICATION WITH DIFFERENT PERSONALITIES.

8: HOW DEPENDABLE DO YOU THINK YOU WERE TODAY? WHY WAS THIS?

9: DID YOU FIND YOURSELF PROCRASTINATING TODAY? HOW COULD YOU CHANGE THIS INTO ACTION?

DATE:-   /   /

1: HOW WAS YOUR DECISION MAKING TODAY, WHY WAS THIS?
WHAT CHANGE COULD YOU MAKE TO MOVE FORWARD INTO TOMORROW?

2: WRITE ONE PROBLEM YOU SOLVED TODAY? HOW DID YOU DEAL
WITH THIS? WHAT COULD YOU DO DIFFERENTLY TO IMPROVE?

3: HOW MUCH EMPATHY HAVE YOU SHOWN TODAY, WHY WAS THIS?
HOW DID YOU FEEL DEALING WITH EMPATHY? THINK ABOUT A CHANGE
TO GROW IN THIS AREA.

4: HOW WAS YOUR PATIENCE TODAY, WHY WAS THIS? WHAT
COULD YOU DO DIFFERENTLY TOMORROW?

5: DID YOU DO ANY MENTORING TODAY, WHY WAS THIS? HOW
COULD YOU DEVELOP THIS AREA?

6: HOW MUCH ACTIVE LISTENING DID YOU DO TODAY? DID YOU ACTUALLY LISTEN TO UNDERSTAND OR LISTEN TO REPLY? HOW COULD YOU IMPROVE ON THIS AREA FOR TOMORROW?

7: HOW WERE YOUR COMMUNICATION SKILLS TODAY? HOW COULD YOU IMPROVE IN THIS AREA? LITTLE CHANGES TO REALLY UNDERSTAND THE HUGE AREA OF COMMUNICATION WITH DIFFERENT PERSONALITIES.

8: HOW DEPENDABLE DO YOU THINK YOU WERE TODAY? WHY WAS THIS?

9: DID YOU FIND YOURSELF PROCRASTINATING TODAY? HOW COULD YOU CHANGE THIS INTO ACTION?

1: HOW HAVE I GROWN OVER THE LAST 10 DAYS

2: WHAT AM I GOING TO FOCUS ON OVER THE NEXT 10 DAYS?

3: WHAT FIVE THINGS AM I POSITIVELY TAKING FROM THE LAST 10 DAYS AND MOVING THEM FORWARD INTO THE NEXT 10 DAYS.

-
-
-
-
-

4: WHAT KEY AREAS WOULD I LIKE TO CONCENTRATE ON?

"Remember managers have subordinates and leaders have followers."

RALPH MOODY

EFFECTIVE LEADER JOURNAL

DATE:-   /   /

1: HOW WAS YOUR DECISION MAKING TODAY, WHY WAS THIS? WHAT CHANGE COULD YOU MAKE TO MOVE FORWARD INTO TOMORROW?

2: WRITE ONE PROBLEM YOU SOLVED TODAY? HOW DID YOU DEAL WITH THIS? WHAT COULD YOU DO DIFFERENTLY TO IMPROVE?

3: HOW MUCH EMPATHY HAVE YOU SHOWN TODAY, WHY WAS THIS? HOW DID YOU FEEL DEALING WITH EMPATHY? THINK ABOUT A CHANGE TO GROW IN THIS AREA.

4: HOW WAS YOUR PATIENCE TODAY, WHY WAS THIS? WHAT COULD YOU DO DIFFERENTLY TOMORROW?

5: DID YOU DO ANY MENTORING TODAY, WHY WAS THIS? HOW COULD YOU DEVELOP THIS AREA?

6: HOW MUCH ACTIVE LISTENING DID YOU DO TODAY? DID YOU ACTUALLY LISTEN TO UNDERSTAND OR LISTEN TO REPLY? HOW COULD YOU IMPROVE ON THIS AREA FOR TOMORROW?

7: HOW WERE YOUR COMMUNICATION SKILLS TODAY? HOW COULD YOU IMPROVE IN THIS AREA? LITTLE CHANGES TO REALLY UNDERSTAND THE HUGE AREA OF COMMUNICATION WITH DIFFERENT PERSONALITIES.

8: HOW DEPENDABLE DO YOU THINK YOU WERE TODAY? WHY WAS THIS?

9: DID YOU FIND YOURSELF PROCRASTINATING TODAY? HOW COULD YOU CHANGE THIS INTO ACTION?

DATE:-   /   /

1: HOW WAS YOUR DECISION MAKING TODAY, WHY WAS THIS? WHAT CHANGE COULD YOU MAKE TO MOVE FORWARD INTO TOMORROW?

2: WRITE ONE PROBLEM YOU SOLVED TODAY? HOW DID YOU DEAL WITH THIS? WHAT COULD YOU DO DIFFERENTLY TO IMPROVE?

3: HOW MUCH EMPATHY HAVE YOU SHOWN TODAY, WHY WAS THIS? HOW DID YOU FEEL DEALING WITH EMPATHY? THINK ABOUT A CHANGE TO GROW IN THIS AREA.

4: HOW WAS YOUR PATIENCE TODAY, WHY WAS THIS? WHAT COULD YOU DO DIFFERENTLY TOMORROW?

5: DID YOU DO ANY MENTORING TODAY, WHY WAS THIS? HOW COULD YOU DEVELOP THIS AREA?

6: HOW MUCH ACTIVE LISTENING DID YOU DO TODAY? DID YOU ACTUALLY LISTEN TO UNDERSTAND OR LISTEN TO REPLY? HOW COULD YOU IMPROVE ON THIS AREA FOR TOMORROW?

7: HOW WERE YOUR COMMUNICATION SKILLS TODAY? HOW COULD YOU IMPROVE IN THIS AREA? LITTLE CHANGES TO REALLY UNDERSTAND THE HUGE AREA OF COMMUNICATION WITH DIFFERENT PERSONALITIES.

8: HOW DEPENDABLE DO YOU THINK YOU WERE TODAY? WHY WAS THIS?

9: DID YOU FIND YOURSELF PROCRASTINATING TODAY? HOW COULD YOU CHANGE THIS INTO ACTION?

DATE:-   /   /

1: HOW WAS YOUR DECISION MAKING TODAY, WHY WAS THIS? WHAT CHANGE COULD YOU MAKE TO MOVE FORWARD INTO TOMORROW?

2: WRITE ONE PROBLEM YOU SOLVED TODAY? HOW DID YOU DEAL WITH THIS? WHAT COULD YOU DO DIFFERENTLY TO IMPROVE?

3: HOW MUCH EMPATHY HAVE YOU SHOWN TODAY, WHY WAS THIS? HOW DID YOU FEEL DEALING WITH EMPATHY? THINK ABOUT A CHANGE TO GROW IN THIS AREA.

4: HOW WAS YOUR PATIENCE TODAY, WHY WAS THIS? WHAT COULD YOU DO DIFFERENTLY TOMORROW?

5: DID YOU DO ANY MENTORING TODAY, WHY WAS THIS? HOW COULD YOU DEVELOP THIS AREA?

6: HOW MUCH ACTIVE LISTENING DID YOU DO TODAY? DID YOU ACTUALLY LISTEN TO UNDERSTAND OR LISTEN TO REPLY? HOW COULD YOU IMPROVE ON THIS AREA FOR TOMORROW?

7: HOW WERE YOUR COMMUNICATION SKILLS TODAY? HOW COULD YOU IMPROVE IN THIS AREA? LITTLE CHANGES TO REALLY UNDERSTAND THE HUGE AREA OF COMMUNICATION WITH DIFFERENT PERSONALITIES.

8: HOW DEPENDABLE DO YOU THINK YOU WERE TODAY? WHY WAS THIS?

9: DID YOU FIND YOURSELF PROCRASTINATING TODAY? HOW COULD YOU CHANGE THIS INTO ACTION?

DATE:-   /   /

1: HOW WAS YOUR DECISION MAKING TODAY, WHY WAS THIS?
WHAT CHANGE COULD YOU MAKE TO MOVE FORWARD INTO TOMORROW?

2: WRITE ONE PROBLEM YOU SOLVED TODAY? HOW DID YOU DEAL
WITH THIS? WHAT COULD YOU DO DIFFERENTLY TO IMPROVE?

3: HOW MUCH EMPATHY HAVE YOU SHOWN TODAY, WHY WAS THIS?
HOW DID YOU FEEL DEALING WITH EMPATHY? THINK ABOUT A CHANGE
TO GROW IN THIS AREA.

4: HOW WAS YOUR PATIENCE TODAY, WHY WAS THIS? WHAT
COULD YOU DO DIFFERENTLY TOMORROW?

5: DID YOU DO ANY MENTORING TODAY, WHY WAS THIS? HOW
COULD YOU DEVELOP THIS AREA?

6: HOW MUCH ACTIVE LISTENING DID YOU DO TODAY? DID YOU ACTUALLY LISTEN TO UNDERSTAND OR LISTEN TO REPLY? HOW COULD YOU IMPROVE ON THIS AREA FOR TOMORROW?

7: HOW WERE YOUR COMMUNICATION SKILLS TODAY? HOW COULD YOU IMPROVE IN THIS AREA? LITTLE CHANGES TO REALLY UNDERSTAND THE HUGE AREA OF COMMUNICATION WITH DIFFERENT PERSONALITIES.

8: HOW DEPENDABLE DO YOU THINK YOU WERE TODAY? WHY WAS THIS?

9: DID YOU FIND YOURSELF PROCRASTINATING TODAY? HOW COULD YOU CHANGE THIS INTO ACTION?

DATE:-   /   /

1: HOW WAS YOUR DECISION MAKING TODAY, WHY WAS THIS? WHAT CHANGE COULD YOU MAKE TO MOVE FORWARD INTO TOMORROW?

2: WRITE ONE PROBLEM YOU SOLVED TODAY? HOW DID YOU DEAL WITH THIS? WHAT COULD YOU DO DIFFERENTLY TO IMPROVE?

3: HOW MUCH EMPATHY HAVE YOU SHOWN TODAY, WHY WAS THIS? HOW DID YOU FEEL DEALING WITH EMPATHY? THINK ABOUT A CHANGE TO GROW IN THIS AREA.

4: HOW WAS YOUR PATIENCE TODAY, WHY WAS THIS? WHAT COULD YOU DO DIFFERENTLY TOMORROW?

5: DID YOU DO ANY MENTORING TODAY, WHY WAS THIS? HOW COULD YOU DEVELOP THIS AREA?

6: HOW MUCH ACTIVE LISTENING DID YOU DO TODAY? DID YOU ACTUALLY LISTEN TO UNDERSTAND OR LISTEN TO REPLY? HOW COULD YOU IMPROVE ON THIS AREA FOR TOMORROW?

7: HOW WERE YOUR COMMUNICATION SKILLS TODAY? HOW COULD YOU IMPROVE IN THIS AREA? LITTLE CHANGES TO REALLY UNDERSTAND THE HUGE AREA OF COMMUNICATION WITH DIFFERENT PERSONALITIES.

8: HOW DEPENDABLE DO YOU THINK YOU WERE TODAY? WHY WAS THIS?

9: DID YOU FIND YOURSELF PROCRASTINATING TODAY? HOW COULD YOU CHANGE THIS INTO ACTION?

DATE:-   /   /

1: HOW WAS YOUR DECISION MAKING TODAY, WHY WAS THIS? WHAT CHANGE COULD YOU MAKE TO MOVE FORWARD INTO TOMORROW?

2: WRITE ONE PROBLEM YOU SOLVED TODAY? HOW DID YOU DEAL WITH THIS? WHAT COULD YOU DO DIFFERENTLY TO IMPROVE?

3: HOW MUCH EMPATHY HAVE YOU SHOWN TODAY, WHY WAS THIS? HOW DID YOU FEEL DEALING WITH EMPATHY? THINK ABOUT A CHANGE TO GROW IN THIS AREA.

4: HOW WAS YOUR PATIENCE TODAY, WHY WAS THIS? WHAT COULD YOU DO DIFFERENTLY TOMORROW?

5: DID YOU DO ANY MENTORING TODAY, WHY WAS THIS? HOW COULD YOU DEVELOP THIS AREA?

6: HOW MUCH ACTIVE LISTENING DID YOU DO TODAY? DID YOU ACTUALLY LISTEN TO UNDERSTAND OR LISTEN TO REPLY? HOW COULD YOU IMPROVE ON THIS AREA FOR TOMORROW?

7: HOW WERE YOUR COMMUNICATION SKILLS TODAY? HOW COULD YOU IMPROVE IN THIS AREA? LITTLE CHANGES TO REALLY UNDERSTAND THE HUGE AREA OF COMMUNICATION WITH DIFFERENT PERSONALITIES.

8: HOW DEPENDABLE DO YOU THINK YOU WERE TODAY? WHY WAS THIS?

9: DID YOU FIND YOURSELF PROCRASTINATING TODAY? HOW COULD YOU CHANGE THIS INTO ACTION?

DATE:-   /   /

1: HOW WAS YOUR DECISION MAKING TODAY, WHY WAS THIS?
WHAT CHANGE COULD YOU MAKE TO MOVE FORWARD INTO TOMORROW?

2: WRITE ONE PROBLEM YOU SOLVED TODAY? HOW DID YOU DEAL
WITH THIS? WHAT COULD YOU DO DIFFERENTLY TO IMPROVE?

3: HOW MUCH EMPATHY HAVE YOU SHOWN TODAY, WHY WAS THIS?
HOW DID YOU FEEL DEALING WITH EMPATHY? THINK ABOUT A CHANGE
TO GROW IN THIS AREA.

4: HOW WAS YOUR PATIENCE TODAY, WHY WAS THIS? WHAT
COULD YOU DO DIFFERENTLY TOMORROW?

5: DID YOU DO ANY MENTORING TODAY, WHY WAS THIS? HOW
COULD YOU DEVELOP THIS AREA?

6: HOW MUCH ACTIVE LISTENING DID YOU DO TODAY? DID YOU ACTUALLY LISTEN TO UNDERSTAND OR LISTEN TO REPLY? HOW COULD YOU IMPROVE ON THIS AREA FOR TOMORROW?

7: HOW WERE YOUR COMMUNICATION SKILLS TODAY? HOW COULD YOU IMPROVE IN THIS AREA? LITTLE CHANGES TO REALLY UNDERSTAND THE HUGE AREA OF COMMUNICATION WITH DIFFERENT PERSONALITIES.

8: HOW DEPENDABLE DO YOU THINK YOU WERE TODAY? WHY WAS THIS?

9: DID YOU FIND YOURSELF PROCRASTINATING TODAY? HOW COULD YOU CHANGE THIS INTO ACTION?

DATE:-   /   /

1: HOW WAS YOUR DECISION MAKING TODAY, WHY WAS THIS?
WHAT CHANGE COULD YOU MAKE TO MOVE FORWARD INTO TOMORROW?

2: WRITE ONE PROBLEM YOU SOLVED TODAY? HOW DID YOU DEAL
WITH THIS? WHAT COULD YOU DO DIFFERENTLY TO IMPROVE?

3: HOW MUCH EMPATHY HAVE YOU SHOWN TODAY, WHY WAS THIS?
HOW DID YOU FEEL DEALING WITH EMPATHY? THINK ABOUT A CHANGE
TO GROW IN THIS AREA.

4: HOW WAS YOUR PATIENCE TODAY, WHY WAS THIS? WHAT
COULD YOU DO DIFFERENTLY TOMORROW?

5: DID YOU DO ANY MENTORING TODAY, WHY WAS THIS? HOW
COULD YOU DEVELOP THIS AREA?

6: HOW MUCH ACTIVE LISTENING DID YOU DO TODAY? DID YOU ACTUALLY LISTEN TO UNDERSTAND OR LISTEN TO REPLY? HOW COULD YOU IMPROVE ON THIS AREA FOR TOMORROW?

7: HOW WERE YOUR COMMUNICATION SKILLS TODAY? HOW COULD YOU IMPROVE IN THIS AREA? LITTLE CHANGES TO REALLY UNDERSTAND THE HUGE AREA OF COMMUNICATION WITH DIFFERENT PERSONALITIES.

8: HOW DEPENDABLE DO YOU THINK YOU WERE TODAY? WHY WAS THIS?

9: DID YOU FIND YOURSELF PROCRASTINATING TODAY? HOW COULD YOU CHANGE THIS INTO ACTION?

DATE:-   /   /

1: HOW WAS YOUR DECISION MAKING TODAY, WHY WAS THIS?
WHAT CHANGE COULD YOU MAKE TO MOVE FORWARD INTO TOMORROW?

2: WRITE ONE PROBLEM YOU SOLVED TODAY? HOW DID YOU DEAL
WITH THIS? WHAT COULD YOU DO DIFFERENTLY TO IMPROVE?

3: HOW MUCH EMPATHY HAVE YOU SHOWN TODAY, WHY WAS THIS?
HOW DID YOU FEEL DEALING WITH EMPATHY? THINK ABOUT A CHANGE
TO GROW IN THIS AREA.

4: HOW WAS YOUR PATIENCE TODAY, WHY WAS THIS? WHAT
COULD YOU DO DIFFERENTLY TOMORROW?

5: DID YOU DO ANY MENTORING TODAY, WHY WAS THIS? HOW
COULD YOU DEVELOP THIS AREA?

6: HOW MUCH ACTIVE LISTENING DID YOU DO TODAY? DID YOU ACTUALLY LISTEN TO UNDERSTAND OR LISTEN TO REPLY? HOW COULD YOU IMPROVE ON THIS AREA FOR TOMORROW?

7: HOW WERE YOUR COMMUNICATION SKILLS TODAY? HOW COULD YOU IMPROVE IN THIS AREA? LITTLE CHANGES TO REALLY UNDERSTAND THE HUGE AREA OF COMMUNICATION WITH DIFFERENT PERSONALITIES.

8: HOW DEPENDABLE DO YOU THINK YOU WERE TODAY? WHY WAS THIS?

9: DID YOU FIND YOURSELF PROCRASTINATING TODAY? HOW COULD YOU CHANGE THIS INTO ACTION?

DATE:-   /   /

1: HOW WAS YOUR DECISION MAKING TODAY, WHY WAS THIS?
WHAT CHANGE COULD YOU MAKE TO MOVE FORWARD INTO TOMORROW?

2: WRITE ONE PROBLEM YOU SOLVED TODAY? HOW DID YOU DEAL
WITH THIS? WHAT COULD YOU DO DIFFERENTLY TO IMPROVE?

3: HOW MUCH EMPATHY HAVE YOU SHOWN TODAY, WHY WAS THIS?
HOW DID YOU FEEL DEALING WITH EMPATHY? THINK ABOUT A CHANGE
TO GROW IN THIS AREA.

4: HOW WAS YOUR PATIENCE TODAY, WHY WAS THIS? WHAT
COULD YOU DO DIFFERENTLY TOMORROW?

5: DID YOU DO ANY MENTORING TODAY, WHY WAS THIS? HOW
COULD YOU DEVELOP THIS AREA?

6: HOW MUCH ACTIVE LISTENING DID YOU DO TODAY? DID YOU ACTUALLY LISTEN TO UNDERSTAND OR LISTEN TO REPLY? HOW COULD YOU IMPROVE ON THIS AREA FOR TOMORROW?

7: HOW WERE YOUR COMMUNICATION SKILLS TODAY? HOW COULD YOU IMPROVE IN THIS AREA? LITTLE CHANGES TO REALLY UNDERSTAND THE HUGE AREA OF COMMUNICATION WITH DIFFERENT PERSONALITIES.

8: HOW DEPENDABLE DO YOU THINK YOU WERE TODAY? WHY WAS THIS?

9: DID YOU FIND YOURSELF PROCRASTINATING TODAY? HOW COULD YOU CHANGE THIS INTO ACTION?

1: HOW HAVE I GROWN OVER THE LAST 10 DAYS

2: WHAT AM I GOING TO FOCUS ON OVER THE NEXT 10 DAYS?

3: WHAT FIVE THINGS AM I POSITIVELY TAKING FROM THE LAST 10 DAYS AND MOVING THEM FORWARD INTO THE NEXT 10 DAYS.

-
-
-
-
-

4: WHAT KEY AREAS WOULD I LIKE TO CONCENTRATE ON?

Exercise One – Think about the differences between leadership and management and think about how you differ in both of these areas.

DATE:-   /   /

1: HOW WAS YOUR DECISION MAKING TODAY, WHY WAS THIS? WHAT CHANGE COULD YOU MAKE TO MOVE FORWARD INTO TOMORROW?

2: WRITE ONE PROBLEM YOU SOLVED TODAY? HOW DID YOU DEAL WITH THIS? WHAT COULD YOU DO DIFFERENTLY TO IMPROVE?

3: HOW MUCH EMPATHY HAVE YOU SHOWN TODAY, WHY WAS THIS? HOW DID YOU FEEL DEALING WITH EMPATHY? THINK ABOUT A CHANGE TO GROW IN THIS AREA.

4: HOW WAS YOUR PATIENCE TODAY, WHY WAS THIS? WHAT COULD YOU DO DIFFERENTLY TOMORROW?

5: DID YOU DO ANY MENTORING TODAY, WHY WAS THIS? HOW COULD YOU DEVELOP THIS AREA?

6: HOW MUCH ACTIVE LISTENING DID YOU DO TODAY? DID YOU ACTUALLY LISTEN TO UNDERSTAND OR LISTEN TO REPLY? HOW COULD YOU IMPROVE ON THIS AREA FOR TOMORROW?

7: HOW WERE YOUR COMMUNICATION SKILLS TODAY? HOW COULD YOU IMPROVE IN THIS AREA? LITTLE CHANGES TO REALLY UNDERSTAND THE HUGE AREA OF COMMUNICATION WITH DIFFERENT PERSONALITIES.

8: HOW DEPENDABLE DO YOU THINK YOU WERE TODAY? WHY WAS THIS?

9: DID YOU FIND YOURSELF PROCRASTINATING TODAY? HOW COULD YOU CHANGE THIS INTO ACTION?

DATE:-   /   /

1: HOW WAS YOUR DECISION MAKING TODAY, WHY WAS THIS?
WHAT CHANGE COULD YOU MAKE TO MOVE FORWARD INTO TOMORROW?

2: WRITE ONE PROBLEM YOU SOLVED TODAY? HOW DID YOU DEAL
WITH THIS? WHAT COULD YOU DO DIFFERENTLY TO IMPROVE?

3: HOW MUCH EMPATHY HAVE YOU SHOWN TODAY, WHY WAS THIS?
HOW DID YOU FEEL DEALING WITH EMPATHY? THINK ABOUT A CHANGE
TO GROW IN THIS AREA.

4: HOW WAS YOUR PATIENCE TODAY, WHY WAS THIS? WHAT
COULD YOU DO DIFFERENTLY TOMORROW?

5: DID YOU DO ANY MENTORING TODAY, WHY WAS THIS? HOW
COULD YOU DEVELOP THIS AREA?

6: HOW MUCH ACTIVE LISTENING DID YOU DO TODAY? DID YOU ACTUALLY LISTEN TO UNDERSTAND OR LISTEN TO REPLY? HOW COULD YOU IMPROVE ON THIS AREA FOR TOMORROW?

7: HOW WERE YOUR COMMUNICATION SKILLS TODAY? HOW COULD YOU IMPROVE IN THIS AREA? LITTLE CHANGES TO REALLY UNDERSTAND THE HUGE AREA OF COMMUNICATION WITH DIFFERENT PERSONALITIES.

8: HOW DEPENDABLE DO YOU THINK YOU WERE TODAY? WHY WAS THIS?

9: DID YOU FIND YOURSELF PROCRASTINATING TODAY? HOW COULD YOU CHANGE THIS INTO ACTION?

DATE:-   /   /

1: HOW WAS YOUR DECISION MAKING TODAY, WHY WAS THIS? WHAT CHANGE COULD YOU MAKE TO MOVE FORWARD INTO TOMORROW?

2: WRITE ONE PROBLEM YOU SOLVED TODAY? HOW DID YOU DEAL WITH THIS? WHAT COULD YOU DO DIFFERENTLY TO IMPROVE?

3: HOW MUCH EMPATHY HAVE YOU SHOWN TODAY, WHY WAS THIS? HOW DID YOU FEEL DEALING WITH EMPATHY? THINK ABOUT A CHANGE TO GROW IN THIS AREA.

4: HOW WAS YOUR PATIENCE TODAY, WHY WAS THIS? WHAT COULD YOU DO DIFFERENTLY TOMORROW?

5: DID YOU DO ANY MENTORING TODAY, WHY WAS THIS? HOW COULD YOU DEVELOP THIS AREA?

6: HOW MUCH ACTIVE LISTENING DID YOU DO TODAY? DID YOU ACTUALLY LISTEN TO UNDERSTAND OR LISTEN TO REPLY? HOW COULD YOU IMPROVE ON THIS AREA FOR TOMORROW?

7: HOW WERE YOUR COMMUNICATION SKILLS TODAY? HOW COULD YOU IMPROVE IN THIS AREA? LITTLE CHANGES TO REALLY UNDERSTAND THE HUGE AREA OF COMMUNICATION WITH DIFFERENT PERSONALITIES.

8: HOW DEPENDABLE DO YOU THINK YOU WERE TODAY? WHY WAS THIS?

9: DID YOU FIND YOURSELF PROCRASTINATING TODAY? HOW COULD YOU CHANGE THIS INTO ACTION?

DATE:-   /   /

1: HOW WAS YOUR DECISION MAKING TODAY, WHY WAS THIS?
WHAT CHANGE COULD YOU MAKE TO MOVE FORWARD INTO TOMORROW?

2: WRITE ONE PROBLEM YOU SOLVED TODAY? HOW DID YOU DEAL
WITH THIS? WHAT COULD YOU DO DIFFERENTLY TO IMPROVE?

3: HOW MUCH EMPATHY HAVE YOU SHOWN TODAY, WHY WAS THIS?
HOW DID YOU FEEL DEALING WITH EMPATHY? THINK ABOUT A CHANGE
TO GROW IN THIS AREA.

4: HOW WAS YOUR PATIENCE TODAY, WHY WAS THIS? WHAT
COULD YOU DO DIFFERENTLY TOMORROW?

5: DID YOU DO ANY MENTORING TODAY, WHY WAS THIS? HOW
COULD YOU DEVELOP THIS AREA?

6: HOW MUCH ACTIVE LISTENING DID YOU DO TODAY? DID YOU ACTUALLY LISTEN TO UNDERSTAND OR LISTEN TO REPLY? HOW COULD YOU IMPROVE ON THIS AREA FOR TOMORROW?

7: HOW WERE YOUR COMMUNICATION SKILLS TODAY? HOW COULD YOU IMPROVE IN THIS AREA? LITTLE CHANGES TO REALLY UNDERSTAND THE HUGE AREA OF COMMUNICATION WITH DIFFERENT PERSONALITIES.

8: HOW DEPENDABLE DO YOU THINK YOU WERE TODAY? WHY WAS THIS?

9: DID YOU FIND YOURSELF PROCRASTINATING TODAY? HOW COULD YOU CHANGE THIS INTO ACTION?

DATE:-   /   /

1: HOW WAS YOUR DECISION MAKING TODAY, WHY WAS THIS? WHAT CHANGE COULD YOU MAKE TO MOVE FORWARD INTO TOMORROW?

2: WRITE ONE PROBLEM YOU SOLVED TODAY? HOW DID YOU DEAL WITH THIS? WHAT COULD YOU DO DIFFERENTLY TO IMPROVE?

3: HOW MUCH EMPATHY HAVE YOU SHOWN TODAY, WHY WAS THIS? HOW DID YOU FEEL DEALING WITH EMPATHY? THINK ABOUT A CHANGE TO GROW IN THIS AREA.

4: HOW WAS YOUR PATIENCE TODAY, WHY WAS THIS? WHAT COULD YOU DO DIFFERENTLY TOMORROW?

5: DID YOU DO ANY MENTORING TODAY, WHY WAS THIS? HOW COULD YOU DEVELOP THIS AREA?

6: HOW MUCH ACTIVE LISTENING DID YOU DO TODAY? DID YOU ACTUALLY LISTEN TO UNDERSTAND OR LISTEN TO REPLY? HOW COULD YOU IMPROVE ON THIS AREA FOR TOMORROW?

7: HOW WERE YOUR COMMUNICATION SKILLS TODAY? HOW COULD YOU IMPROVE IN THIS AREA? LITTLE CHANGES TO REALLY UNDERSTAND THE HUGE AREA OF COMMUNICATION WITH DIFFERENT PERSONALITIES.

8: HOW DEPENDABLE DO YOU THINK YOU WERE TODAY? WHY WAS THIS?

9: DID YOU FIND YOURSELF PROCRASTINATING TODAY? HOW COULD YOU CHANGE THIS INTO ACTION?

DATE:-   /   /

1: HOW WAS YOUR DECISION MAKING TODAY, WHY WAS THIS?
WHAT CHANGE COULD YOU MAKE TO MOVE FORWARD INTO TOMORROW?

2: WRITE ONE PROBLEM YOU SOLVED TODAY? HOW DID YOU DEAL
WITH THIS? WHAT COULD YOU DO DIFFERENTLY TO IMPROVE?

3: HOW MUCH EMPATHY HAVE YOU SHOWN TODAY, WHY WAS THIS?
HOW DID YOU FEEL DEALING WITH EMPATHY? THINK ABOUT A CHANGE
TO GROW IN THIS AREA.

4: HOW WAS YOUR PATIENCE TODAY, WHY WAS THIS? WHAT
COULD YOU DO DIFFERENTLY TOMORROW?

5: DID YOU DO ANY MENTORING TODAY, WHY WAS THIS? HOW
COULD YOU DEVELOP THIS AREA?

6: HOW MUCH ACTIVE LISTENING DID YOU DO TODAY? DID YOU ACTUALLY LISTEN TO UNDERSTAND OR LISTEN TO REPLY? HOW COULD YOU IMPROVE ON THIS AREA FOR TOMORROW?

7: HOW WERE YOUR COMMUNICATION SKILLS TODAY? HOW COULD YOU IMPROVE IN THIS AREA? LITTLE CHANGES TO REALLY UNDERSTAND THE HUGE AREA OF COMMUNICATION WITH DIFFERENT PERSONALITIES.

8: HOW DEPENDABLE DO YOU THINK YOU WERE TODAY? WHY WAS THIS?

9: DID YOU FIND YOURSELF PROCRASTINATING TODAY? HOW COULD YOU CHANGE THIS INTO ACTION?

DATE:-   /   /

1: HOW WAS YOUR DECISION MAKING TODAY, WHY WAS THIS? WHAT CHANGE COULD YOU MAKE TO MOVE FORWARD INTO TOMORROW?

2: WRITE ONE PROBLEM YOU SOLVED TODAY? HOW DID YOU DEAL WITH THIS? WHAT COULD YOU DO DIFFERENTLY TO IMPROVE?

3: HOW MUCH EMPATHY HAVE YOU SHOWN TODAY, WHY WAS THIS? HOW DID YOU FEEL DEALING WITH EMPATHY? THINK ABOUT A CHANGE TO GROW IN THIS AREA.

4: HOW WAS YOUR PATIENCE TODAY, WHY WAS THIS? WHAT COULD YOU DO DIFFERENTLY TOMORROW?

5: DID YOU DO ANY MENTORING TODAY, WHY WAS THIS? HOW COULD YOU DEVELOP THIS AREA?

6: HOW MUCH ACTIVE LISTENING DID YOU DO TODAY? DID YOU ACTUALLY LISTEN TO UNDERSTAND OR LISTEN TO REPLY? HOW COULD YOU IMPROVE ON THIS AREA FOR TOMORROW?

7: HOW WERE YOUR COMMUNICATION SKILLS TODAY? HOW COULD YOU IMPROVE IN THIS AREA? LITTLE CHANGES TO REALLY UNDERSTAND THE HUGE AREA OF COMMUNICATION WITH DIFFERENT PERSONALITIES.

8: HOW DEPENDABLE DO YOU THINK YOU WERE TODAY? WHY WAS THIS?

9: DID YOU FIND YOURSELF PROCRASTINATING TODAY? HOW COULD YOU CHANGE THIS INTO ACTION?

DATE:-   /   /

1: HOW WAS YOUR DECISION MAKING TODAY, WHY WAS THIS?
WHAT CHANGE COULD YOU MAKE TO MOVE FORWARD INTO TOMORROW?

2: WRITE ONE PROBLEM YOU SOLVED TODAY? HOW DID YOU DEAL
WITH THIS? WHAT COULD YOU DO DIFFERENTLY TO IMPROVE?

3: HOW MUCH EMPATHY HAVE YOU SHOWN TODAY, WHY WAS THIS?
HOW DID YOU FEEL DEALING WITH EMPATHY? THINK ABOUT A CHANGE
TO GROW IN THIS AREA.

4: HOW WAS YOUR PATIENCE TODAY, WHY WAS THIS? WHAT
COULD YOU DO DIFFERENTLY TOMORROW?

5: DID YOU DO ANY MENTORING TODAY, WHY WAS THIS? HOW
COULD YOU DEVELOP THIS AREA?

6: HOW MUCH ACTIVE LISTENING DID YOU DO TODAY? DID YOU ACTUALLY LISTEN TO UNDERSTAND OR LISTEN TO REPLY? HOW COULD YOU IMPROVE ON THIS AREA FOR TOMORROW?

7: HOW WERE YOUR COMMUNICATION SKILLS TODAY? HOW COULD YOU IMPROVE IN THIS AREA? LITTLE CHANGES TO REALLY UNDERSTAND THE HUGE AREA OF COMMUNICATION WITH DIFFERENT PERSONALITIES.

8: HOW DEPENDABLE DO YOU THINK YOU WERE TODAY? WHY WAS THIS?

9: DID YOU FIND YOURSELF PROCRASTINATING TODAY? HOW COULD YOU CHANGE THIS INTO ACTION?

DATE:-   /   /

1: HOW WAS YOUR DECISION MAKING TODAY, WHY WAS THIS? WHAT CHANGE COULD YOU MAKE TO MOVE FORWARD INTO TOMORROW?

2: WRITE ONE PROBLEM YOU SOLVED TODAY? HOW DID YOU DEAL WITH THIS? WHAT COULD YOU DO DIFFERENTLY TO IMPROVE?

3: HOW MUCH EMPATHY HAVE YOU SHOWN TODAY, WHY WAS THIS? HOW DID YOU FEEL DEALING WITH EMPATHY? THINK ABOUT A CHANGE TO GROW IN THIS AREA.

4: HOW WAS YOUR PATIENCE TODAY, WHY WAS THIS? WHAT COULD YOU DO DIFFERENTLY TOMORROW?

5: DID YOU DO ANY MENTORING TODAY, WHY WAS THIS? HOW COULD YOU DEVELOP THIS AREA?

6: HOW MUCH ACTIVE LISTENING DID YOU DO TODAY? DID YOU ACTUALLY LISTEN TO UNDERSTAND OR LISTEN TO REPLY? HOW COULD YOU IMPROVE ON THIS AREA FOR TOMORROW?

7: HOW WERE YOUR COMMUNICATION SKILLS TODAY? HOW COULD YOU IMPROVE IN THIS AREA? LITTLE CHANGES TO REALLY UNDERSTAND THE HUGE AREA OF COMMUNICATION WITH DIFFERENT PERSONALITIES.

8: HOW DEPENDABLE DO YOU THINK YOU WERE TODAY? WHY WAS THIS?

9: DID YOU FIND YOURSELF PROCRASTINATING TODAY? HOW COULD YOU CHANGE THIS INTO ACTION?

DATE:-   /   /

1: HOW WAS YOUR DECISION MAKING TODAY, WHY WAS THIS? WHAT CHANGE COULD YOU MAKE TO MOVE FORWARD INTO TOMORROW?

2: WRITE ONE PROBLEM YOU SOLVED TODAY? HOW DID YOU DEAL WITH THIS? WHAT COULD YOU DO DIFFERENTLY TO IMPROVE?

3: HOW MUCH EMPATHY HAVE YOU SHOWN TODAY, WHY WAS THIS? HOW DID YOU FEEL DEALING WITH EMPATHY? THINK ABOUT A CHANGE TO GROW IN THIS AREA.

4: HOW WAS YOUR PATIENCE TODAY, WHY WAS THIS? WHAT COULD YOU DO DIFFERENTLY TOMORROW?

5: DID YOU DO ANY MENTORING TODAY, WHY WAS THIS? HOW COULD YOU DEVELOP THIS AREA?

6: HOW MUCH ACTIVE LISTENING DID YOU DO TODAY? DID YOU ACTUALLY LISTEN TO UNDERSTAND OR LISTEN TO REPLY? HOW COULD YOU IMPROVE ON THIS AREA FOR TOMORROW?

7: HOW WERE YOUR COMMUNICATION SKILLS TODAY? HOW COULD YOU IMPROVE IN THIS AREA? LITTLE CHANGES TO REALLY UNDERSTAND THE HUGE AREA OF COMMUNICATION WITH DIFFERENT PERSONALITIES.

8: HOW DEPENDABLE DO YOU THINK YOU WERE TODAY? WHY WAS THIS?

9: DID YOU FIND YOURSELF PROCRASTINATING TODAY? HOW COULD YOU CHANGE THIS INTO ACTION?

1: HOW HAVE I GROWN OVER THE LAST 10 DAYS

2: WHAT AM I GOING TO FOCUS ON OVER THE NEXT 10 DAYS?

3: WHAT FIVE THINGS AM I POSITIVELY TAKING FROM THE LAST 10 DAYS AND MOVING THEM FORWARD INTO THE NEXT 10 DAYS.

-
-
-
-
-

4: WHAT KEY AREAS WOULD I LIKE TO CONCENTRATE ON?

Day 50 Congratulations

Congratulations for meeting the halfway point, tremendous effort and fantastic that you are reflecting effectively. The book is for you only, very personnel and as you reflect on the last fifty days, look at your incredible journey. Every little change is the change you need to move forward. Think about achieving your goal of improving and what will it feel like at day 100, just imagine that feeling.

DATE:-   /   /

1: HOW WAS YOUR DECISION MAKING TODAY, WHY WAS THIS? WHAT CHANGE COULD YOU MAKE TO MOVE FORWARD INTO TOMORROW?

2: WRITE ONE PROBLEM YOU SOLVED TODAY? HOW DID YOU DEAL WITH THIS? WHAT COULD YOU DO DIFFERENTLY TO IMPROVE?

3: HOW MUCH EMPATHY HAVE YOU SHOWN TODAY, WHY WAS THIS? HOW DID YOU FEEL DEALING WITH EMPATHY? THINK ABOUT A CHANGE TO GROW IN THIS AREA.

4: HOW WAS YOUR PATIENCE TODAY, WHY WAS THIS? WHAT COULD YOU DO DIFFERENTLY TOMORROW?

5: DID YOU DO ANY MENTORING TODAY, WHY WAS THIS? HOW COULD YOU DEVELOP THIS AREA?

6: HOW MUCH ACTIVE LISTENING DID YOU DO TODAY? DID YOU ACTUALLY LISTEN TO UNDERSTAND OR LISTEN TO REPLY? HOW COULD YOU IMPROVE ON THIS AREA FOR TOMORROW?

7: HOW WERE YOUR COMMUNICATION SKILLS TODAY? HOW COULD YOU IMPROVE IN THIS AREA? LITTLE CHANGES TO REALLY UNDERSTAND THE HUGE AREA OF COMMUNICATION WITH DIFFERENT PERSONALITIES.

8: HOW DEPENDABLE DO YOU THINK YOU WERE TODAY? WHY WAS THIS?

9: DID YOU FIND YOURSELF PROCRASTINATING TODAY? HOW COULD YOU CHANGE THIS INTO ACTION?

DATE:-   /   /

1: HOW WAS YOUR DECISION MAKING TODAY, WHY WAS THIS?
WHAT CHANGE COULD YOU MAKE TO MOVE FORWARD INTO TOMORROW?

2: WRITE ONE PROBLEM YOU SOLVED TODAY? HOW DID YOU DEAL
WITH THIS? WHAT COULD YOU DO DIFFERENTLY TO IMPROVE?

3: HOW MUCH EMPATHY HAVE YOU SHOWN TODAY, WHY WAS THIS?
HOW DID YOU FEEL DEALING WITH EMPATHY? THINK ABOUT A CHANGE
TO GROW IN THIS AREA.

4: HOW WAS YOUR PATIENCE TODAY, WHY WAS THIS? WHAT
COULD YOU DO DIFFERENTLY TOMORROW?

5: DID YOU DO ANY MENTORING TODAY, WHY WAS THIS? HOW
COULD YOU DEVELOP THIS AREA?

6: HOW MUCH ACTIVE LISTENING DID YOU DO TODAY? DID YOU ACTUALLY LISTEN TO UNDERSTAND OR LISTEN TO REPLY? HOW COULD YOU IMPROVE ON THIS AREA FOR TOMORROW?

7: HOW WERE YOUR COMMUNICATION SKILLS TODAY? HOW COULD YOU IMPROVE IN THIS AREA? LITTLE CHANGES TO REALLY UNDERSTAND THE HUGE AREA OF COMMUNICATION WITH DIFFERENT PERSONALITIES.

8: HOW DEPENDABLE DO YOU THINK YOU WERE TODAY? WHY WAS THIS?

9: DID YOU FIND YOURSELF PROCRASTINATING TODAY? HOW COULD YOU CHANGE THIS INTO ACTION?

DATE:-   /   /

1: HOW WAS YOUR DECISION MAKING TODAY, WHY WAS THIS?
WHAT CHANGE COULD YOU MAKE TO MOVE FORWARD INTO TOMORROW?

2: WRITE ONE PROBLEM YOU SOLVED TODAY? HOW DID YOU DEAL
WITH THIS? WHAT COULD YOU DO DIFFERENTLY TO IMPROVE?

3: HOW MUCH EMPATHY HAVE YOU SHOWN TODAY, WHY WAS THIS?
HOW DID YOU FEEL DEALING WITH EMPATHY? THINK ABOUT A CHANGE
TO GROW IN THIS AREA.

4: HOW WAS YOUR PATIENCE TODAY, WHY WAS THIS? WHAT
COULD YOU DO DIFFERENTLY TOMORROW?

5: DID YOU DO ANY MENTORING TODAY, WHY WAS THIS? HOW
COULD YOU DEVELOP THIS AREA?

6: HOW MUCH ACTIVE LISTENING DID YOU DO TODAY? DID YOU ACTUALLY LISTEN TO UNDERSTAND OR LISTEN TO REPLY? HOW COULD YOU IMPROVE ON THIS AREA FOR TOMORROW?

7: HOW WERE YOUR COMMUNICATION SKILLS TODAY? HOW COULD YOU IMPROVE IN THIS AREA? LITTLE CHANGES TO REALLY UNDERSTAND THE HUGE AREA OF COMMUNICATION WITH DIFFERENT PERSONALITIES.

8: HOW DEPENDABLE DO YOU THINK YOU WERE TODAY? WHY WAS THIS?

9: DID YOU FIND YOURSELF PROCRASTINATING TODAY? HOW COULD YOU CHANGE THIS INTO ACTION?

DATE:-   /   /

1: HOW WAS YOUR DECISION MAKING TODAY, WHY WAS THIS? WHAT CHANGE COULD YOU MAKE TO MOVE FORWARD INTO TOMORROW?

2: WRITE ONE PROBLEM YOU SOLVED TODAY? HOW DID YOU DEAL WITH THIS? WHAT COULD YOU DO DIFFERENTLY TO IMPROVE?

3: HOW MUCH EMPATHY HAVE YOU SHOWN TODAY, WHY WAS THIS? HOW DID YOU FEEL DEALING WITH EMPATHY? THINK ABOUT A CHANGE TO GROW IN THIS AREA.

4: HOW WAS YOUR PATIENCE TODAY, WHY WAS THIS? WHAT COULD YOU DO DIFFERENTLY TOMORROW?

5: DID YOU DO ANY MENTORING TODAY, WHY WAS THIS? HOW COULD YOU DEVELOP THIS AREA?

6: HOW MUCH ACTIVE LISTENING DID YOU DO TODAY? DID YOU ACTUALLY LISTEN TO UNDERSTAND OR LISTEN TO REPLY? HOW COULD YOU IMPROVE ON THIS AREA FOR TOMORROW?

7: HOW WERE YOUR COMMUNICATION SKILLS TODAY? HOW COULD YOU IMPROVE IN THIS AREA? LITTLE CHANGES TO REALLY UNDERSTAND THE HUGE AREA OF COMMUNICATION WITH DIFFERENT PERSONALITIES.

8: HOW DEPENDABLE DO YOU THINK YOU WERE TODAY? WHY WAS THIS?

9: DID YOU FIND YOURSELF PROCRASTINATING TODAY? HOW COULD YOU CHANGE THIS INTO ACTION?

DATE:-   /   /

1: HOW WAS YOUR DECISION MAKING TODAY, WHY WAS THIS? WHAT CHANGE COULD YOU MAKE TO MOVE FORWARD INTO TOMORROW?

2: WRITE ONE PROBLEM YOU SOLVED TODAY? HOW DID YOU DEAL WITH THIS? WHAT COULD YOU DO DIFFERENTLY TO IMPROVE?

3: HOW MUCH EMPATHY HAVE YOU SHOWN TODAY, WHY WAS THIS? HOW DID YOU FEEL DEALING WITH EMPATHY? THINK ABOUT A CHANGE TO GROW IN THIS AREA.

4: HOW WAS YOUR PATIENCE TODAY, WHY WAS THIS? WHAT COULD YOU DO DIFFERENTLY TOMORROW?

5: DID YOU DO ANY MENTORING TODAY, WHY WAS THIS? HOW COULD YOU DEVELOP THIS AREA?

6: HOW MUCH ACTIVE LISTENING DID YOU DO TODAY? DID YOU ACTUALLY LISTEN TO UNDERSTAND OR LISTEN TO REPLY? HOW COULD YOU IMPROVE ON THIS AREA FOR TOMORROW?

7: HOW WERE YOUR COMMUNICATION SKILLS TODAY? HOW COULD YOU IMPROVE IN THIS AREA? LITTLE CHANGES TO REALLY UNDERSTAND THE HUGE AREA OF COMMUNICATION WITH DIFFERENT PERSONALITIES.

8: HOW DEPENDABLE DO YOU THINK YOU WERE TODAY? WHY WAS THIS?

9: DID YOU FIND YOURSELF PROCRASTINATING TODAY? HOW COULD YOU CHANGE THIS INTO ACTION?

DATE:-   /   /

1: HOW WAS YOUR DECISION MAKING TODAY, WHY WAS THIS? WHAT CHANGE COULD YOU MAKE TO MOVE FORWARD INTO TOMORROW?

2: WRITE ONE PROBLEM YOU SOLVED TODAY? HOW DID YOU DEAL WITH THIS? WHAT COULD YOU DO DIFFERENTLY TO IMPROVE?

3: HOW MUCH EMPATHY HAVE YOU SHOWN TODAY, WHY WAS THIS? HOW DID YOU FEEL DEALING WITH EMPATHY? THINK ABOUT A CHANGE TO GROW IN THIS AREA.

4: HOW WAS YOUR PATIENCE TODAY, WHY WAS THIS? WHAT COULD YOU DO DIFFERENTLY TOMORROW?

5: DID YOU DO ANY MENTORING TODAY, WHY WAS THIS? HOW COULD YOU DEVELOP THIS AREA?

6: HOW MUCH ACTIVE LISTENING DID YOU DO TODAY? DID YOU ACTUALLY LISTEN TO UNDERSTAND OR LISTEN TO REPLY? HOW COULD YOU IMPROVE ON THIS AREA FOR TOMORROW?

7: HOW WERE YOUR COMMUNICATION SKILLS TODAY? HOW COULD YOU IMPROVE IN THIS AREA? LITTLE CHANGES TO REALLY UNDERSTAND THE HUGE AREA OF COMMUNICATION WITH DIFFERENT PERSONALITIES.

8: HOW DEPENDABLE DO YOU THINK YOU WERE TODAY? WHY WAS THIS?

9: DID YOU FIND YOURSELF PROCRASTINATING TODAY? HOW COULD YOU CHANGE THIS INTO ACTION?

DATE:-   /   /

1: HOW WAS YOUR DECISION MAKING TODAY, WHY WAS THIS? WHAT CHANGE COULD YOU MAKE TO MOVE FORWARD INTO TOMORROW?

2: WRITE ONE PROBLEM YOU SOLVED TODAY? HOW DID YOU DEAL WITH THIS? WHAT COULD YOU DO DIFFERENTLY TO IMPROVE?

3: HOW MUCH EMPATHY HAVE YOU SHOWN TODAY, WHY WAS THIS? HOW DID YOU FEEL DEALING WITH EMPATHY? THINK ABOUT A CHANGE TO GROW IN THIS AREA.

4: HOW WAS YOUR PATIENCE TODAY, WHY WAS THIS? WHAT COULD YOU DO DIFFERENTLY TOMORROW?

5: DID YOU DO ANY MENTORING TODAY, WHY WAS THIS? HOW COULD YOU DEVELOP THIS AREA?

6: HOW MUCH ACTIVE LISTENING DID YOU DO TODAY? DID YOU ACTUALLY LISTEN TO UNDERSTAND OR LISTEN TO REPLY? HOW COULD YOU IMPROVE ON THIS AREA FOR TOMORROW?

7: HOW WERE YOUR COMMUNICATION SKILLS TODAY? HOW COULD YOU IMPROVE IN THIS AREA? LITTLE CHANGES TO REALLY UNDERSTAND THE HUGE AREA OF COMMUNICATION WITH DIFFERENT PERSONALITIES.

8: HOW DEPENDABLE DO YOU THINK YOU WERE TODAY? WHY WAS THIS?

9: DID YOU FIND YOURSELF PROCRASTINATING TODAY? HOW COULD YOU CHANGE THIS INTO ACTION?

DATE:-   /   /

1: HOW WAS YOUR DECISION MAKING TODAY, WHY WAS THIS? WHAT CHANGE COULD YOU MAKE TO MOVE FORWARD INTO TOMORROW?

2: WRITE ONE PROBLEM YOU SOLVED TODAY? HOW DID YOU DEAL WITH THIS? WHAT COULD YOU DO DIFFERENTLY TO IMPROVE?

3: HOW MUCH EMPATHY HAVE YOU SHOWN TODAY, WHY WAS THIS? HOW DID YOU FEEL DEALING WITH EMPATHY? THINK ABOUT A CHANGE TO GROW IN THIS AREA.

4: HOW WAS YOUR PATIENCE TODAY, WHY WAS THIS? WHAT COULD YOU DO DIFFERENTLY TOMORROW?

5: DID YOU DO ANY MENTORING TODAY, WHY WAS THIS? HOW COULD YOU DEVELOP THIS AREA?

6: HOW MUCH ACTIVE LISTENING DID YOU DO TODAY? DID YOU ACTUALLY LISTEN TO UNDERSTAND OR LISTEN TO REPLY? HOW COULD YOU IMPROVE ON THIS AREA FOR TOMORROW?

7: HOW WERE YOUR COMMUNICATION SKILLS TODAY? HOW COULD YOU IMPROVE IN THIS AREA? LITTLE CHANGES TO REALLY UNDERSTAND THE HUGE AREA OF COMMUNICATION WITH DIFFERENT PERSONALITIES.

8: HOW DEPENDABLE DO YOU THINK YOU WERE TODAY? WHY WAS THIS?

9: DID YOU FIND YOURSELF PROCRASTINATING TODAY? HOW COULD YOU CHANGE THIS INTO ACTION?

DATE:-   /   /

1: HOW WAS YOUR DECISION MAKING TODAY, WHY WAS THIS?
WHAT CHANGE COULD YOU MAKE TO MOVE FORWARD INTO TOMORROW?

2: WRITE ONE PROBLEM YOU SOLVED TODAY? HOW DID YOU DEAL
WITH THIS? WHAT COULD YOU DO DIFFERENTLY TO IMPROVE?

3: HOW MUCH EMPATHY HAVE YOU SHOWN TODAY, WHY WAS THIS?
HOW DID YOU FEEL DEALING WITH EMPATHY? THINK ABOUT A CHANGE
TO GROW IN THIS AREA.

4: HOW WAS YOUR PATIENCE TODAY, WHY WAS THIS? WHAT
COULD YOU DO DIFFERENTLY TOMORROW?

5: DID YOU DO ANY MENTORING TODAY, WHY WAS THIS? HOW
COULD YOU DEVELOP THIS AREA?

6: HOW MUCH ACTIVE LISTENING DID YOU DO TODAY? DID YOU ACTUALLY LISTEN TO UNDERSTAND OR LISTEN TO REPLY? HOW COULD YOU IMPROVE ON THIS AREA FOR TOMORROW?

7: HOW WERE YOUR COMMUNICATION SKILLS TODAY? HOW COULD YOU IMPROVE IN THIS AREA? LITTLE CHANGES TO REALLY UNDERSTAND THE HUGE AREA OF COMMUNICATION WITH DIFFERENT PERSONALITIES.

8: HOW DEPENDABLE DO YOU THINK YOU WERE TODAY? WHY WAS THIS?

9: DID YOU FIND YOURSELF PROCRASTINATING TODAY? HOW COULD YOU CHANGE THIS INTO ACTION?

DATE:-   /   /

1: HOW WAS YOUR DECISION MAKING TODAY, WHY WAS THIS? WHAT CHANGE COULD YOU MAKE TO MOVE FORWARD INTO TOMORROW?

2: WRITE ONE PROBLEM YOU SOLVED TODAY? HOW DID YOU DEAL WITH THIS? WHAT COULD YOU DO DIFFERENTLY TO IMPROVE?

3: HOW MUCH EMPATHY HAVE YOU SHOWN TODAY, WHY WAS THIS? HOW DID YOU FEEL DEALING WITH EMPATHY? THINK ABOUT A CHANGE TO GROW IN THIS AREA.

4: HOW WAS YOUR PATIENCE TODAY, WHY WAS THIS? WHAT COULD YOU DO DIFFERENTLY TOMORROW?

5: DID YOU DO ANY MENTORING TODAY, WHY WAS THIS? HOW COULD YOU DEVELOP THIS AREA?

6: HOW MUCH ACTIVE LISTENING DID YOU DO TODAY? DID YOU ACTUALLY LISTEN TO UNDERSTAND OR LISTEN TO REPLY? HOW COULD YOU IMPROVE ON THIS AREA FOR TOMORROW?

7: HOW WERE YOUR COMMUNICATION SKILLS TODAY? HOW COULD YOU IMPROVE IN THIS AREA? LITTLE CHANGES TO REALLY UNDERSTAND THE HUGE AREA OF COMMUNICATION WITH DIFFERENT PERSONALITIES.

8: HOW DEPENDABLE DO YOU THINK YOU WERE TODAY? WHY WAS THIS?

9: DID YOU FIND YOURSELF PROCRASTINATING TODAY? HOW COULD YOU CHANGE THIS INTO ACTION?

1: HOW HAVE I GROWN OVER THE LAST 10 DAYS

2: WHAT AM I GOING TO FOCUS ON OVER THE NEXT 10 DAYS?

3: WHAT FIVE THINGS AM I POSITIVELY TAKING FROM THE LAST 10 DAYS AND MOVING THEM FORWARD INTO THE NEXT 10 DAYS.

-
-
-
-
-

4: WHAT KEY AREAS WOULD I LIKE TO CONCENTRATE ON?

Exercise Two, write your strengths then write your areas for improvement, 5 of each.

DATE:-   /   /

1: HOW WAS YOUR DECISION MAKING TODAY, WHY WAS THIS?
WHAT CHANGE COULD YOU MAKE TO MOVE FORWARD INTO TOMORROW?

2: WRITE ONE PROBLEM YOU SOLVED TODAY? HOW DID YOU DEAL
WITH THIS? WHAT COULD YOU DO DIFFERENTLY TO IMPROVE?

3: HOW MUCH EMPATHY HAVE YOU SHOWN TODAY, WHY WAS THIS?
HOW DID YOU FEEL DEALING WITH EMPATHY? THINK ABOUT A CHANGE
TO GROW IN THIS AREA.

4: HOW WAS YOUR PATIENCE TODAY, WHY WAS THIS? WHAT
COULD YOU DO DIFFERENTLY TOMORROW?

5: DID YOU DO ANY MENTORING TODAY, WHY WAS THIS? HOW
COULD YOU DEVELOP THIS AREA?

6: HOW MUCH ACTIVE LISTENING DID YOU DO TODAY? DID YOU ACTUALLY LISTEN TO UNDERSTAND OR LISTEN TO REPLY? HOW COULD YOU IMPROVE ON THIS AREA FOR TOMORROW?

7: HOW WERE YOUR COMMUNICATION SKILLS TODAY? HOW COULD YOU IMPROVE IN THIS AREA? LITTLE CHANGES TO REALLY UNDERSTAND THE HUGE AREA OF COMMUNICATION WITH DIFFERENT PERSONALITIES.

8: HOW DEPENDABLE DO YOU THINK YOU WERE TODAY? WHY WAS THIS?

9: DID YOU FIND YOURSELF PROCRASTINATING TODAY? HOW COULD YOU CHANGE THIS INTO ACTION?

DATE:-   /   /

1: HOW WAS YOUR DECISION MAKING TODAY, WHY WAS THIS? WHAT CHANGE COULD YOU MAKE TO MOVE FORWARD INTO TOMORROW?

2: WRITE ONE PROBLEM YOU SOLVED TODAY? HOW DID YOU DEAL WITH THIS? WHAT COULD YOU DO DIFFERENTLY TO IMPROVE?

3: HOW MUCH EMPATHY HAVE YOU SHOWN TODAY, WHY WAS THIS? HOW DID YOU FEEL DEALING WITH EMPATHY? THINK ABOUT A CHANGE TO GROW IN THIS AREA.

4: HOW WAS YOUR PATIENCE TODAY, WHY WAS THIS? WHAT COULD YOU DO DIFFERENTLY TOMORROW?

5: DID YOU DO ANY MENTORING TODAY, WHY WAS THIS? HOW COULD YOU DEVELOP THIS AREA?

6: HOW MUCH ACTIVE LISTENING DID YOU DO TODAY? DID YOU ACTUALLY LISTEN TO UNDERSTAND OR LISTEN TO REPLY? HOW COULD YOU IMPROVE ON THIS AREA FOR TOMORROW?

7: HOW WERE YOUR COMMUNICATION SKILLS TODAY? HOW COULD YOU IMPROVE IN THIS AREA? LITTLE CHANGES TO REALLY UNDERSTAND THE HUGE AREA OF COMMUNICATION WITH DIFFERENT PERSONALITIES.

8: HOW DEPENDABLE DO YOU THINK YOU WERE TODAY? WHY WAS THIS?

9: DID YOU FIND YOURSELF PROCRASTINATING TODAY? HOW COULD YOU CHANGE THIS INTO ACTION?

DATE:-   /   /

1: HOW WAS YOUR DECISION MAKING TODAY, WHY WAS THIS? WHAT CHANGE COULD YOU MAKE TO MOVE FORWARD INTO TOMORROW?

2: WRITE ONE PROBLEM YOU SOLVED TODAY? HOW DID YOU DEAL WITH THIS? WHAT COULD YOU DO DIFFERENTLY TO IMPROVE?

3: HOW MUCH EMPATHY HAVE YOU SHOWN TODAY, WHY WAS THIS? HOW DID YOU FEEL DEALING WITH EMPATHY? THINK ABOUT A CHANGE TO GROW IN THIS AREA.

4: HOW WAS YOUR PATIENCE TODAY, WHY WAS THIS? WHAT COULD YOU DO DIFFERENTLY TOMORROW?

5: DID YOU DO ANY MENTORING TODAY, WHY WAS THIS? HOW COULD YOU DEVELOP THIS AREA?

6: HOW MUCH ACTIVE LISTENING DID YOU DO TODAY? DID YOU ACTUALLY LISTEN TO UNDERSTAND OR LISTEN TO REPLY? HOW COULD YOU IMPROVE ON THIS AREA FOR TOMORROW?

7: HOW WERE YOUR COMMUNICATION SKILLS TODAY? HOW COULD YOU IMPROVE IN THIS AREA? LITTLE CHANGES TO REALLY UNDERSTAND THE HUGE AREA OF COMMUNICATION WITH DIFFERENT PERSONALITIES.

8: HOW DEPENDABLE DO YOU THINK YOU WERE TODAY? WHY WAS THIS?

9: DID YOU FIND YOURSELF PROCRASTINATING TODAY? HOW COULD YOU CHANGE THIS INTO ACTION?

DATE:-   /   /

1: HOW WAS YOUR DECISION MAKING TODAY, WHY WAS THIS? WHAT CHANGE COULD YOU MAKE TO MOVE FORWARD INTO TOMORROW?

2: WRITE ONE PROBLEM YOU SOLVED TODAY? HOW DID YOU DEAL WITH THIS? WHAT COULD YOU DO DIFFERENTLY TO IMPROVE?

3: HOW MUCH EMPATHY HAVE YOU SHOWN TODAY, WHY WAS THIS? HOW DID YOU FEEL DEALING WITH EMPATHY? THINK ABOUT A CHANGE TO GROW IN THIS AREA.

4: HOW WAS YOUR PATIENCE TODAY, WHY WAS THIS? WHAT COULD YOU DO DIFFERENTLY TOMORROW?

5: DID YOU DO ANY MENTORING TODAY, WHY WAS THIS? HOW COULD YOU DEVELOP THIS AREA?

6: HOW MUCH ACTIVE LISTENING DID YOU DO TODAY? DID YOU ACTUALLY LISTEN TO UNDERSTAND OR LISTEN TO REPLY? HOW COULD YOU IMPROVE ON THIS AREA FOR TOMORROW?

7: HOW WERE YOUR COMMUNICATION SKILLS TODAY? HOW COULD YOU IMPROVE IN THIS AREA? LITTLE CHANGES TO REALLY UNDERSTAND THE HUGE AREA OF COMMUNICATION WITH DIFFERENT PERSONALITIES.

8: HOW DEPENDABLE DO YOU THINK YOU WERE TODAY? WHY WAS THIS?

9: DID YOU FIND YOURSELF PROCRASTINATING TODAY? HOW COULD YOU CHANGE THIS INTO ACTION?

DATE:-   /   /

1: HOW WAS YOUR DECISION MAKING TODAY, WHY WAS THIS? WHAT CHANGE COULD YOU MAKE TO MOVE FORWARD INTO TOMORROW?

2: WRITE ONE PROBLEM YOU SOLVED TODAY? HOW DID YOU DEAL WITH THIS? WHAT COULD YOU DO DIFFERENTLY TO IMPROVE?

3: HOW MUCH EMPATHY HAVE YOU SHOWN TODAY, WHY WAS THIS? HOW DID YOU FEEL DEALING WITH EMPATHY? THINK ABOUT A CHANGE TO GROW IN THIS AREA.

4: HOW WAS YOUR PATIENCE TODAY, WHY WAS THIS? WHAT COULD YOU DO DIFFERENTLY TOMORROW?

5: DID YOU DO ANY MENTORING TODAY, WHY WAS THIS? HOW COULD YOU DEVELOP THIS AREA?

6: HOW MUCH ACTIVE LISTENING DID YOU DO TODAY? DID YOU ACTUALLY LISTEN TO UNDERSTAND OR LISTEN TO REPLY? HOW COULD YOU IMPROVE ON THIS AREA FOR TOMORROW?

7: HOW WERE YOUR COMMUNICATION SKILLS TODAY? HOW COULD YOU IMPROVE IN THIS AREA? LITTLE CHANGES TO REALLY UNDERSTAND THE HUGE AREA OF COMMUNICATION WITH DIFFERENT PERSONALITIES.

8: HOW DEPENDABLE DO YOU THINK YOU WERE TODAY? WHY WAS THIS?

9: DID YOU FIND YOURSELF PROCRASTINATING TODAY? HOW COULD YOU CHANGE THIS INTO ACTION?

DATE:-   /   /

1: HOW WAS YOUR DECISION MAKING TODAY, WHY WAS THIS? WHAT CHANGE COULD YOU MAKE TO MOVE FORWARD INTO TOMORROW?

2: WRITE ONE PROBLEM YOU SOLVED TODAY? HOW DID YOU DEAL WITH THIS? WHAT COULD YOU DO DIFFERENTLY TO IMPROVE?

3: HOW MUCH EMPATHY HAVE YOU SHOWN TODAY, WHY WAS THIS? HOW DID YOU FEEL DEALING WITH EMPATHY? THINK ABOUT A CHANGE TO GROW IN THIS AREA.

4: HOW WAS YOUR PATIENCE TODAY, WHY WAS THIS? WHAT COULD YOU DO DIFFERENTLY TOMORROW?

5: DID YOU DO ANY MENTORING TODAY, WHY WAS THIS? HOW COULD YOU DEVELOP THIS AREA?

6: HOW MUCH ACTIVE LISTENING DID YOU DO TODAY? DID YOU ACTUALLY LISTEN TO UNDERSTAND OR LISTEN TO REPLY? HOW COULD YOU IMPROVE ON THIS AREA FOR TOMORROW?

7: HOW WERE YOUR COMMUNICATION SKILLS TODAY? HOW COULD YOU IMPROVE IN THIS AREA? LITTLE CHANGES TO REALLY UNDERSTAND THE HUGE AREA OF COMMUNICATION WITH DIFFERENT PERSONALITIES.

8: HOW DEPENDABLE DO YOU THINK YOU WERE TODAY? WHY WAS THIS?

9: DID YOU FIND YOURSELF PROCRASTINATING TODAY? HOW COULD YOU CHANGE THIS INTO ACTION?

DATE:-   /   /

1: HOW WAS YOUR DECISION MAKING TODAY, WHY WAS THIS?
WHAT CHANGE COULD YOU MAKE TO MOVE FORWARD INTO TOMORROW?

2: WRITE ONE PROBLEM YOU SOLVED TODAY? HOW DID YOU DEAL
WITH THIS? WHAT COULD YOU DO DIFFERENTLY TO IMPROVE?

3: HOW MUCH EMPATHY HAVE YOU SHOWN TODAY, WHY WAS THIS?
HOW DID YOU FEEL DEALING WITH EMPATHY? THINK ABOUT A CHANGE
TO GROW IN THIS AREA.

4: HOW WAS YOUR PATIENCE TODAY, WHY WAS THIS? WHAT
COULD YOU DO DIFFERENTLY TOMORROW?

5: DID YOU DO ANY MENTORING TODAY, WHY WAS THIS? HOW
COULD YOU DEVELOP THIS AREA?

6: HOW MUCH ACTIVE LISTENING DID YOU DO TODAY? DID YOU ACTUALLY LISTEN TO UNDERSTAND OR LISTEN TO REPLY? HOW COULD YOU IMPROVE ON THIS AREA FOR TOMORROW?

7: HOW WERE YOUR COMMUNICATION SKILLS TODAY? HOW COULD YOU IMPROVE IN THIS AREA? LITTLE CHANGES TO REALLY UNDERSTAND THE HUGE AREA OF COMMUNICATION WITH DIFFERENT PERSONALITIES.

8: HOW DEPENDABLE DO YOU THINK YOU WERE TODAY? WHY WAS THIS?

9: DID YOU FIND YOURSELF PROCRASTINATING TODAY? HOW COULD YOU CHANGE THIS INTO ACTION?

DATE:-   /   /

1: HOW WAS YOUR DECISION MAKING TODAY, WHY WAS THIS?
WHAT CHANGE COULD YOU MAKE TO MOVE FORWARD INTO TOMORROW?

2: WRITE ONE PROBLEM YOU SOLVED TODAY? HOW DID YOU DEAL
WITH THIS? WHAT COULD YOU DO DIFFERENTLY TO IMPROVE?

3: HOW MUCH EMPATHY HAVE YOU SHOWN TODAY, WHY WAS THIS?
HOW DID YOU FEEL DEALING WITH EMPATHY? THINK ABOUT A CHANGE
TO GROW IN THIS AREA.

4: HOW WAS YOUR PATIENCE TODAY, WHY WAS THIS? WHAT
COULD YOU DO DIFFERENTLY TOMORROW?

5: DID YOU DO ANY MENTORING TODAY, WHY WAS THIS? HOW
COULD YOU DEVELOP THIS AREA?

6: HOW MUCH ACTIVE LISTENING DID YOU DO TODAY? DID YOU ACTUALLY LISTEN TO UNDERSTAND OR LISTEN TO REPLY? HOW COULD YOU IMPROVE ON THIS AREA FOR TOMORROW?

7: HOW WERE YOUR COMMUNICATION SKILLS TODAY? HOW COULD YOU IMPROVE IN THIS AREA? LITTLE CHANGES TO REALLY UNDERSTAND THE HUGE AREA OF COMMUNICATION WITH DIFFERENT PERSONALITIES.

8: HOW DEPENDABLE DO YOU THINK YOU WERE TODAY? WHY WAS THIS?

9: DID YOU FIND YOURSELF PROCRASTINATING TODAY? HOW COULD YOU CHANGE THIS INTO ACTION?

DATE:-   /   /

1: HOW WAS YOUR DECISION MAKING TODAY, WHY WAS THIS?
WHAT CHANGE COULD YOU MAKE TO MOVE FORWARD INTO TOMORROW?

2: WRITE ONE PROBLEM YOU SOLVED TODAY? HOW DID YOU DEAL
WITH THIS? WHAT COULD YOU DO DIFFERENTLY TO IMPROVE?

3: HOW MUCH EMPATHY HAVE YOU SHOWN TODAY, WHY WAS THIS?
HOW DID YOU FEEL DEALING WITH EMPATHY? THINK ABOUT A CHANGE
TO GROW IN THIS AREA.

4: HOW WAS YOUR PATIENCE TODAY, WHY WAS THIS? WHAT
COULD YOU DO DIFFERENTLY TOMORROW?

5: DID YOU DO ANY MENTORING TODAY, WHY WAS THIS? HOW
COULD YOU DEVELOP THIS AREA?

6: HOW MUCH ACTIVE LISTENING DID YOU DO TODAY? DID YOU ACTUALLY LISTEN TO UNDERSTAND OR LISTEN TO REPLY? HOW COULD YOU IMPROVE ON THIS AREA FOR TOMORROW?

7: HOW WERE YOUR COMMUNICATION SKILLS TODAY? HOW COULD YOU IMPROVE IN THIS AREA? LITTLE CHANGES TO REALLY UNDERSTAND THE HUGE AREA OF COMMUNICATION WITH DIFFERENT PERSONALITIES.

8: HOW DEPENDABLE DO YOU THINK YOU WERE TODAY? WHY WAS THIS?

9: DID YOU FIND YOURSELF PROCRASTINATING TODAY? HOW COULD YOU CHANGE THIS INTO ACTION?

DATE:-   /   /

1: HOW WAS YOUR DECISION MAKING TODAY, WHY WAS THIS?
WHAT CHANGE COULD YOU MAKE TO MOVE FORWARD INTO TOMORROW?

2: WRITE ONE PROBLEM YOU SOLVED TODAY? HOW DID YOU DEAL
WITH THIS? WHAT COULD YOU DO DIFFERENTLY TO IMPROVE?

3: HOW MUCH EMPATHY HAVE YOU SHOWN TODAY, WHY WAS THIS?
HOW DID YOU FEEL DEALING WITH EMPATHY? THINK ABOUT A CHANGE
TO GROW IN THIS AREA.

4: HOW WAS YOUR PATIENCE TODAY, WHY WAS THIS? WHAT
COULD YOU DO DIFFERENTLY TOMORROW?

5: DID YOU DO ANY MENTORING TODAY, WHY WAS THIS? HOW
COULD YOU DEVELOP THIS AREA?

6: HOW MUCH ACTIVE LISTENING DID YOU DO TODAY? DID YOU ACTUALLY LISTEN TO UNDERSTAND OR LISTEN TO REPLY? HOW COULD YOU IMPROVE ON THIS AREA FOR TOMORROW?

7: HOW WERE YOUR COMMUNICATION SKILLS TODAY? HOW COULD YOU IMPROVE IN THIS AREA? LITTLE CHANGES TO REALLY UNDERSTAND THE HUGE AREA OF COMMUNICATION WITH DIFFERENT PERSONALITIES.

8: HOW DEPENDABLE DO YOU THINK YOU WERE TODAY? WHY WAS THIS?

9: DID YOU FIND YOURSELF PROCRASTINATING TODAY? HOW COULD YOU CHANGE THIS INTO ACTION?

1: HOW HAVE I GROWN OVER THE LAST 10 DAYS

2: WHAT AM I GOING TO FOCUS ON OVER THE NEXT 10 DAYS?

3: WHAT FIVE THINGS AM I POSITIVELY TAKING FROM THE LAST 10 DAYS AND MOVING THEM FORWARD INTO THE NEXT 10 DAYS.

-
-
-
-
-

4: WHAT KEY AREAS WOULD I LIKE TO CONCENTRATE ON?

"Think about the best leader you know, then live like them for a day."

CLAIRE MOODY

DATE:-   /   /

1: HOW WAS YOUR DECISION MAKING TODAY, WHY WAS THIS? WHAT CHANGE COULD YOU MAKE TO MOVE FORWARD INTO TOMORROW?

2: WRITE ONE PROBLEM YOU SOLVED TODAY? HOW DID YOU DEAL WITH THIS? WHAT COULD YOU DO DIFFERENTLY TO IMPROVE?

3: HOW MUCH EMPATHY HAVE YOU SHOWN TODAY, WHY WAS THIS? HOW DID YOU FEEL DEALING WITH EMPATHY? THINK ABOUT A CHANGE TO GROW IN THIS AREA.

4: HOW WAS YOUR PATIENCE TODAY, WHY WAS THIS? WHAT COULD YOU DO DIFFERENTLY TOMORROW?

5: DID YOU DO ANY MENTORING TODAY, WHY WAS THIS? HOW COULD YOU DEVELOP THIS AREA?

6: HOW MUCH ACTIVE LISTENING DID YOU DO TODAY? DID YOU ACTUALLY LISTEN TO UNDERSTAND OR LISTEN TO REPLY? HOW COULD YOU IMPROVE ON THIS AREA FOR TOMORROW?

7: HOW WERE YOUR COMMUNICATION SKILLS TODAY? HOW COULD YOU IMPROVE IN THIS AREA? LITTLE CHANGES TO REALLY UNDERSTAND THE HUGE AREA OF COMMUNICATION WITH DIFFERENT PERSONALITIES.

8: HOW DEPENDABLE DO YOU THINK YOU WERE TODAY? WHY WAS THIS?

9: DID YOU FIND YOURSELF PROCRASTINATING TODAY? HOW COULD YOU CHANGE THIS INTO ACTION?

DATE:-   /   /

1: HOW WAS YOUR DECISION MAKING TODAY, WHY WAS THIS? WHAT CHANGE COULD YOU MAKE TO MOVE FORWARD INTO TOMORROW?

2: WRITE ONE PROBLEM YOU SOLVED TODAY? HOW DID YOU DEAL WITH THIS? WHAT COULD YOU DO DIFFERENTLY TO IMPROVE?

3: HOW MUCH EMPATHY HAVE YOU SHOWN TODAY, WHY WAS THIS? HOW DID YOU FEEL DEALING WITH EMPATHY? THINK ABOUT A CHANGE TO GROW IN THIS AREA.

4: HOW WAS YOUR PATIENCE TODAY, WHY WAS THIS? WHAT COULD YOU DO DIFFERENTLY TOMORROW?

5: DID YOU DO ANY MENTORING TODAY, WHY WAS THIS? HOW COULD YOU DEVELOP THIS AREA?

6: HOW MUCH ACTIVE LISTENING DID YOU DO TODAY? DID YOU ACTUALLY LISTEN TO UNDERSTAND OR LISTEN TO REPLY? HOW COULD YOU IMPROVE ON THIS AREA FOR TOMORROW?

7: HOW WERE YOUR COMMUNICATION SKILLS TODAY? HOW COULD YOU IMPROVE IN THIS AREA? LITTLE CHANGES TO REALLY UNDERSTAND THE HUGE AREA OF COMMUNICATION WITH DIFFERENT PERSONALITIES.

8: HOW DEPENDABLE DO YOU THINK YOU WERE TODAY? WHY WAS THIS?

9: DID YOU FIND YOURSELF PROCRASTINATING TODAY? HOW COULD YOU CHANGE THIS INTO ACTION?

DATE:-   /   /

1: HOW WAS YOUR DECISION MAKING TODAY, WHY WAS THIS? WHAT CHANGE COULD YOU MAKE TO MOVE FORWARD INTO TOMORROW?

2: WRITE ONE PROBLEM YOU SOLVED TODAY? HOW DID YOU DEAL WITH THIS? WHAT COULD YOU DO DIFFERENTLY TO IMPROVE?

3: HOW MUCH EMPATHY HAVE YOU SHOWN TODAY, WHY WAS THIS? HOW DID YOU FEEL DEALING WITH EMPATHY? THINK ABOUT A CHANGE TO GROW IN THIS AREA.

4: HOW WAS YOUR PATIENCE TODAY, WHY WAS THIS? WHAT COULD YOU DO DIFFERENTLY TOMORROW?

5: DID YOU DO ANY MENTORING TODAY, WHY WAS THIS? HOW COULD YOU DEVELOP THIS AREA?

6: HOW MUCH ACTIVE LISTENING DID YOU DO TODAY? DID YOU ACTUALLY LISTEN TO UNDERSTAND OR LISTEN TO REPLY? HOW COULD YOU IMPROVE ON THIS AREA FOR TOMORROW?

7: HOW WERE YOUR COMMUNICATION SKILLS TODAY? HOW COULD YOU IMPROVE IN THIS AREA? LITTLE CHANGES TO REALLY UNDERSTAND THE HUGE AREA OF COMMUNICATION WITH DIFFERENT PERSONALITIES.

8: HOW DEPENDABLE DO YOU THINK YOU WERE TODAY? WHY WAS THIS?

9: DID YOU FIND YOURSELF PROCRASTINATING TODAY? HOW COULD YOU CHANGE THIS INTO ACTION?

DATE:-   /   /

1: HOW WAS YOUR DECISION MAKING TODAY, WHY WAS THIS? WHAT CHANGE COULD YOU MAKE TO MOVE FORWARD INTO TOMORROW?

2: WRITE ONE PROBLEM YOU SOLVED TODAY? HOW DID YOU DEAL WITH THIS? WHAT COULD YOU DO DIFFERENTLY TO IMPROVE?

3: HOW MUCH EMPATHY HAVE YOU SHOWN TODAY, WHY WAS THIS? HOW DID YOU FEEL DEALING WITH EMPATHY? THINK ABOUT A CHANGE TO GROW IN THIS AREA.

4: HOW WAS YOUR PATIENCE TODAY, WHY WAS THIS? WHAT COULD YOU DO DIFFERENTLY TOMORROW?

5: DID YOU DO ANY MENTORING TODAY, WHY WAS THIS? HOW COULD YOU DEVELOP THIS AREA?

6: HOW MUCH ACTIVE LISTENING DID YOU DO TODAY? DID YOU ACTUALLY LISTEN TO UNDERSTAND OR LISTEN TO REPLY? HOW COULD YOU IMPROVE ON THIS AREA FOR TOMORROW?

7: HOW WERE YOUR COMMUNICATION SKILLS TODAY? HOW COULD YOU IMPROVE IN THIS AREA? LITTLE CHANGES TO REALLY UNDERSTAND THE HUGE AREA OF COMMUNICATION WITH DIFFERENT PERSONALITIES.

8: HOW DEPENDABLE DO YOU THINK YOU WERE TODAY? WHY WAS THIS?

9: DID YOU FIND YOURSELF PROCRASTINATING TODAY? HOW COULD YOU CHANGE THIS INTO ACTION?

DATE:-   /   /

1: HOW WAS YOUR DECISION MAKING TODAY, WHY WAS THIS? WHAT CHANGE COULD YOU MAKE TO MOVE FORWARD INTO TOMORROW?

2: WRITE ONE PROBLEM YOU SOLVED TODAY? HOW DID YOU DEAL WITH THIS? WHAT COULD YOU DO DIFFERENTLY TO IMPROVE?

3: HOW MUCH EMPATHY HAVE YOU SHOWN TODAY, WHY WAS THIS? HOW DID YOU FEEL DEALING WITH EMPATHY? THINK ABOUT A CHANGE TO GROW IN THIS AREA.

4: HOW WAS YOUR PATIENCE TODAY, WHY WAS THIS? WHAT COULD YOU DO DIFFERENTLY TOMORROW?

5: DID YOU DO ANY MENTORING TODAY, WHY WAS THIS? HOW COULD YOU DEVELOP THIS AREA?

6: HOW MUCH ACTIVE LISTENING DID YOU DO TODAY? DID YOU ACTUALLY LISTEN TO UNDERSTAND OR LISTEN TO REPLY? HOW COULD YOU IMPROVE ON THIS AREA FOR TOMORROW?

7: HOW WERE YOUR COMMUNICATION SKILLS TODAY? HOW COULD YOU IMPROVE IN THIS AREA? LITTLE CHANGES TO REALLY UNDERSTAND THE HUGE AREA OF COMMUNICATION WITH DIFFERENT PERSONALITIES.

8: HOW DEPENDABLE DO YOU THINK YOU WERE TODAY? WHY WAS THIS?

9: DID YOU FIND YOURSELF PROCRASTINATING TODAY? HOW COULD YOU CHANGE THIS INTO ACTION?

DATE:-   /   /

1: HOW WAS YOUR DECISION MAKING TODAY, WHY WAS THIS?
WHAT CHANGE COULD YOU MAKE TO MOVE FORWARD INTO TOMORROW?

2: WRITE ONE PROBLEM YOU SOLVED TODAY? HOW DID YOU DEAL
WITH THIS? WHAT COULD YOU DO DIFFERENTLY TO IMPROVE?

3: HOW MUCH EMPATHY HAVE YOU SHOWN TODAY, WHY WAS THIS?
HOW DID YOU FEEL DEALING WITH EMPATHY? THINK ABOUT A CHANGE
TO GROW IN THIS AREA.

4: HOW WAS YOUR PATIENCE TODAY, WHY WAS THIS? WHAT
COULD YOU DO DIFFERENTLY TOMORROW?

5: DID YOU DO ANY MENTORING TODAY, WHY WAS THIS? HOW
COULD YOU DEVELOP THIS AREA?

6: HOW MUCH ACTIVE LISTENING DID YOU DO TODAY? DID YOU ACTUALLY LISTEN TO UNDERSTAND OR LISTEN TO REPLY? HOW COULD YOU IMPROVE ON THIS AREA FOR TOMORROW?

7: HOW WERE YOUR COMMUNICATION SKILLS TODAY? HOW COULD YOU IMPROVE IN THIS AREA? LITTLE CHANGES TO REALLY UNDERSTAND THE HUGE AREA OF COMMUNICATION WITH DIFFERENT PERSONALITIES.

8: HOW DEPENDABLE DO YOU THINK YOU WERE TODAY? WHY WAS THIS?

9: DID YOU FIND YOURSELF PROCRASTINATING TODAY? HOW COULD YOU CHANGE THIS INTO ACTION?

DATE:-   /   /

1: HOW WAS YOUR DECISION MAKING TODAY, WHY WAS THIS? WHAT CHANGE COULD YOU MAKE TO MOVE FORWARD INTO TOMORROW?

2: WRITE ONE PROBLEM YOU SOLVED TODAY? HOW DID YOU DEAL WITH THIS? WHAT COULD YOU DO DIFFERENTLY TO IMPROVE?

3: HOW MUCH EMPATHY HAVE YOU SHOWN TODAY, WHY WAS THIS? HOW DID YOU FEEL DEALING WITH EMPATHY? THINK ABOUT A CHANGE TO GROW IN THIS AREA.

4: HOW WAS YOUR PATIENCE TODAY, WHY WAS THIS? WHAT COULD YOU DO DIFFERENTLY TOMORROW?

5: DID YOU DO ANY MENTORING TODAY, WHY WAS THIS? HOW COULD YOU DEVELOP THIS AREA?

6: HOW MUCH ACTIVE LISTENING DID YOU DO TODAY? DID YOU ACTUALLY LISTEN TO UNDERSTAND OR LISTEN TO REPLY? HOW COULD YOU IMPROVE ON THIS AREA FOR TOMORROW?

7: HOW WERE YOUR COMMUNICATION SKILLS TODAY? HOW COULD YOU IMPROVE IN THIS AREA? LITTLE CHANGES TO REALLY UNDERSTAND THE HUGE AREA OF COMMUNICATION WITH DIFFERENT PERSONALITIES.

8: HOW DEPENDABLE DO YOU THINK YOU WERE TODAY? WHY WAS THIS?

9: DID YOU FIND YOURSELF PROCRASTINATING TODAY? HOW COULD YOU CHANGE THIS INTO ACTION?

DATE:-   /   /

1: HOW WAS YOUR DECISION MAKING TODAY, WHY WAS THIS? WHAT CHANGE COULD YOU MAKE TO MOVE FORWARD INTO TOMORROW?

2: WRITE ONE PROBLEM YOU SOLVED TODAY? HOW DID YOU DEAL WITH THIS? WHAT COULD YOU DO DIFFERENTLY TO IMPROVE?

3: HOW MUCH EMPATHY HAVE YOU SHOWN TODAY, WHY WAS THIS? HOW DID YOU FEEL DEALING WITH EMPATHY? THINK ABOUT A CHANGE TO GROW IN THIS AREA.

4: HOW WAS YOUR PATIENCE TODAY, WHY WAS THIS? WHAT COULD YOU DO DIFFERENTLY TOMORROW?

5: DID YOU DO ANY MENTORING TODAY, WHY WAS THIS? HOW COULD YOU DEVELOP THIS AREA?

6: HOW MUCH ACTIVE LISTENING DID YOU DO TODAY? DID YOU ACTUALLY LISTEN TO UNDERSTAND OR LISTEN TO REPLY? HOW COULD YOU IMPROVE ON THIS AREA FOR TOMORROW?

7: HOW WERE YOUR COMMUNICATION SKILLS TODAY? HOW COULD YOU IMPROVE IN THIS AREA? LITTLE CHANGES TO REALLY UNDERSTAND THE HUGE AREA OF COMMUNICATION WITH DIFFERENT PERSONALITIES.

8: HOW DEPENDABLE DO YOU THINK YOU WERE TODAY? WHY WAS THIS?

9: DID YOU FIND YOURSELF PROCRASTINATING TODAY? HOW COULD YOU CHANGE THIS INTO ACTION?

DATE:-   /   /

1: HOW WAS YOUR DECISION MAKING TODAY, WHY WAS THIS? WHAT CHANGE COULD YOU MAKE TO MOVE FORWARD INTO TOMORROW?

2: WRITE ONE PROBLEM YOU SOLVED TODAY? HOW DID YOU DEAL WITH THIS? WHAT COULD YOU DO DIFFERENTLY TO IMPROVE?

3: HOW MUCH EMPATHY HAVE YOU SHOWN TODAY, WHY WAS THIS? HOW DID YOU FEEL DEALING WITH EMPATHY? THINK ABOUT A CHANGE TO GROW IN THIS AREA.

4: HOW WAS YOUR PATIENCE TODAY, WHY WAS THIS? WHAT COULD YOU DO DIFFERENTLY TOMORROW?

5: DID YOU DO ANY MENTORING TODAY, WHY WAS THIS? HOW COULD YOU DEVELOP THIS AREA?

6: HOW MUCH ACTIVE LISTENING DID YOU DO TODAY? DID YOU ACTUALLY LISTEN TO UNDERSTAND OR LISTEN TO REPLY? HOW COULD YOU IMPROVE ON THIS AREA FOR TOMORROW?

7: HOW WERE YOUR COMMUNICATION SKILLS TODAY? HOW COULD YOU IMPROVE IN THIS AREA? LITTLE CHANGES TO REALLY UNDERSTAND THE HUGE AREA OF COMMUNICATION WITH DIFFERENT PERSONALITIES.

8: HOW DEPENDABLE DO YOU THINK YOU WERE TODAY? WHY WAS THIS?

9: DID YOU FIND YOURSELF PROCRASTINATING TODAY? HOW COULD YOU CHANGE THIS INTO ACTION?

DATE:-   /   /

1: HOW WAS YOUR DECISION MAKING TODAY, WHY WAS THIS? WHAT CHANGE COULD YOU MAKE TO MOVE FORWARD INTO TOMORROW?

2: WRITE ONE PROBLEM YOU SOLVED TODAY? HOW DID YOU DEAL WITH THIS? WHAT COULD YOU DO DIFFERENTLY TO IMPROVE?

3: HOW MUCH EMPATHY HAVE YOU SHOWN TODAY, WHY WAS THIS? HOW DID YOU FEEL DEALING WITH EMPATHY? THINK ABOUT A CHANGE TO GROW IN THIS AREA.

4: HOW WAS YOUR PATIENCE TODAY, WHY WAS THIS? WHAT COULD YOU DO DIFFERENTLY TOMORROW?

5: DID YOU DO ANY MENTORING TODAY, WHY WAS THIS? HOW COULD YOU DEVELOP THIS AREA?

6: HOW MUCH ACTIVE LISTENING DID YOU DO TODAY? DID YOU ACTUALLY LISTEN TO UNDERSTAND OR LISTEN TO REPLY? HOW COULD YOU IMPROVE ON THIS AREA FOR TOMORROW?

7: HOW WERE YOUR COMMUNICATION SKILLS TODAY? HOW COULD YOU IMPROVE IN THIS AREA? LITTLE CHANGES TO REALLY UNDERSTAND THE HUGE AREA OF COMMUNICATION WITH DIFFERENT PERSONALITIES.

8: HOW DEPENDABLE DO YOU THINK YOU WERE TODAY? WHY WAS THIS?

9: DID YOU FIND YOURSELF PROCRASTINATING TODAY? HOW COULD YOU CHANGE THIS INTO ACTION?

EFFECTIVE LEADER JOURNAL

DAY 71 - 80
REVIEW

1: HOW HAVE I GROWN OVER THE LAST 10 DAYS

2: WHAT AM I GOING TO FOCUS ON OVER THE NEXT 10 DAYS?

3: WHAT FIVE THINGS AM I POSITIVELY TAKING FROM THE LAST 10 DAYS AND MOVING THEM FORWARD INTO THE NEXT 10 DAYS.

-
-
-
-
-

4: WHAT KEY AREAS WOULD I LIKE TO CONCENTRATE ON?

"Managers tell the vision and leaders sell the vision. Managers make decisions and leaders facilitate them."

RALPH MOODY

DATE:-   /   /

1: HOW WAS YOUR DECISION MAKING TODAY, WHY WAS THIS? WHAT CHANGE COULD YOU MAKE TO MOVE FORWARD INTO TOMORROW?

2: WRITE ONE PROBLEM YOU SOLVED TODAY? HOW DID YOU DEAL WITH THIS? WHAT COULD YOU DO DIFFERENTLY TO IMPROVE?

3: HOW MUCH EMPATHY HAVE YOU SHOWN TODAY, WHY WAS THIS? HOW DID YOU FEEL DEALING WITH EMPATHY? THINK ABOUT A CHANGE TO GROW IN THIS AREA.

4: HOW WAS YOUR PATIENCE TODAY, WHY WAS THIS? WHAT COULD YOU DO DIFFERENTLY TOMORROW?

5: DID YOU DO ANY MENTORING TODAY, WHY WAS THIS? HOW COULD YOU DEVELOP THIS AREA?

6: HOW MUCH ACTIVE LISTENING DID YOU DO TODAY? DID YOU ACTUALLY LISTEN TO UNDERSTAND OR LISTEN TO REPLY? HOW COULD YOU IMPROVE ON THIS AREA FOR TOMORROW?

7: HOW WERE YOUR COMMUNICATION SKILLS TODAY? HOW COULD YOU IMPROVE IN THIS AREA? LITTLE CHANGES TO REALLY UNDERSTAND THE HUGE AREA OF COMMUNICATION WITH DIFFERENT PERSONALITIES.

8: HOW DEPENDABLE DO YOU THINK YOU WERE TODAY? WHY WAS THIS?

9: DID YOU FIND YOURSELF PROCRASTINATING TODAY? HOW COULD YOU CHANGE THIS INTO ACTION?

DATE:-   /   /

1: HOW WAS YOUR DECISION MAKING TODAY, WHY WAS THIS?
WHAT CHANGE COULD YOU MAKE TO MOVE FORWARD INTO TOMORROW?

2: WRITE ONE PROBLEM YOU SOLVED TODAY? HOW DID YOU DEAL
WITH THIS? WHAT COULD YOU DO DIFFERENTLY TO IMPROVE?

3: HOW MUCH EMPATHY HAVE YOU SHOWN TODAY, WHY WAS THIS?
HOW DID YOU FEEL DEALING WITH EMPATHY? THINK ABOUT A CHANGE
TO GROW IN THIS AREA.

4: HOW WAS YOUR PATIENCE TODAY, WHY WAS THIS? WHAT
COULD YOU DO DIFFERENTLY TOMORROW?

5: DID YOU DO ANY MENTORING TODAY, WHY WAS THIS? HOW
COULD YOU DEVELOP THIS AREA?

6: HOW MUCH ACTIVE LISTENING DID YOU DO TODAY? DID YOU ACTUALLY LISTEN TO UNDERSTAND OR LISTEN TO REPLY? HOW COULD YOU IMPROVE ON THIS AREA FOR TOMORROW?

7: HOW WERE YOUR COMMUNICATION SKILLS TODAY? HOW COULD YOU IMPROVE IN THIS AREA? LITTLE CHANGES TO REALLY UNDERSTAND THE HUGE AREA OF COMMUNICATION WITH DIFFERENT PERSONALITIES.

8: HOW DEPENDABLE DO YOU THINK YOU WERE TODAY? WHY WAS THIS?

9: DID YOU FIND YOURSELF PROCRASTINATING TODAY? HOW COULD YOU CHANGE THIS INTO ACTION?

DATE:-   /   /

1: HOW WAS YOUR DECISION MAKING TODAY, WHY WAS THIS?
WHAT CHANGE COULD YOU MAKE TO MOVE FORWARD INTO TOMORROW?

2: WRITE ONE PROBLEM YOU SOLVED TODAY? HOW DID YOU DEAL
WITH THIS? WHAT COULD YOU DO DIFFERENTLY TO IMPROVE?

3: HOW MUCH EMPATHY HAVE YOU SHOWN TODAY, WHY WAS THIS?
HOW DID YOU FEEL DEALING WITH EMPATHY? THINK ABOUT A CHANGE
TO GROW IN THIS AREA.

4: HOW WAS YOUR PATIENCE TODAY, WHY WAS THIS? WHAT
COULD YOU DO DIFFERENTLY TOMORROW?

5: DID YOU DO ANY MENTORING TODAY, WHY WAS THIS? HOW
COULD YOU DEVELOP THIS AREA?

6: HOW MUCH ACTIVE LISTENING DID YOU DO TODAY? DID YOU ACTUALLY LISTEN TO UNDERSTAND OR LISTEN TO REPLY? HOW COULD YOU IMPROVE ON THIS AREA FOR TOMORROW?

7: HOW WERE YOUR COMMUNICATION SKILLS TODAY? HOW COULD YOU IMPROVE IN THIS AREA? LITTLE CHANGES TO REALLY UNDERSTAND THE HUGE AREA OF COMMUNICATION WITH DIFFERENT PERSONALITIES.

8: HOW DEPENDABLE DO YOU THINK YOU WERE TODAY? WHY WAS THIS?

9: DID YOU FIND YOURSELF PROCRASTINATING TODAY? HOW COULD YOU CHANGE THIS INTO ACTION?

DATE:-   /   /

1: HOW WAS YOUR DECISION MAKING TODAY, WHY WAS THIS? WHAT CHANGE COULD YOU MAKE TO MOVE FORWARD INTO TOMORROW?

2: WRITE ONE PROBLEM YOU SOLVED TODAY? HOW DID YOU DEAL WITH THIS? WHAT COULD YOU DO DIFFERENTLY TO IMPROVE?

3: HOW MUCH EMPATHY HAVE YOU SHOWN TODAY, WHY WAS THIS? HOW DID YOU FEEL DEALING WITH EMPATHY? THINK ABOUT A CHANGE TO GROW IN THIS AREA.

4: HOW WAS YOUR PATIENCE TODAY, WHY WAS THIS? WHAT COULD YOU DO DIFFERENTLY TOMORROW?

5: DID YOU DO ANY MENTORING TODAY, WHY WAS THIS? HOW COULD YOU DEVELOP THIS AREA?

6: HOW MUCH ACTIVE LISTENING DID YOU DO TODAY? DID YOU ACTUALLY LISTEN TO UNDERSTAND OR LISTEN TO REPLY? HOW COULD YOU IMPROVE ON THIS AREA FOR TOMORROW?

7: HOW WERE YOUR COMMUNICATION SKILLS TODAY? HOW COULD YOU IMPROVE IN THIS AREA? LITTLE CHANGES TO REALLY UNDERSTAND THE HUGE AREA OF COMMUNICATION WITH DIFFERENT PERSONALITIES.

8: HOW DEPENDABLE DO YOU THINK YOU WERE TODAY? WHY WAS THIS?

9: DID YOU FIND YOURSELF PROCRASTINATING TODAY? HOW COULD YOU CHANGE THIS INTO ACTION?

DATE:-   /   /

**1: HOW WAS YOUR DECISION MAKING TODAY, WHY WAS THIS?
WHAT CHANGE COULD YOU MAKE TO MOVE FORWARD INTO TOMORROW?**

**2: WRITE ONE PROBLEM YOU SOLVED TODAY? HOW DID YOU DEAL
WITH THIS? WHAT COULD YOU DO DIFFERENTLY TO IMPROVE?**

**3: HOW MUCH EMPATHY HAVE YOU SHOWN TODAY, WHY WAS THIS?
HOW DID YOU FEEL DEALING WITH EMPATHY? THINK ABOUT A CHANGE
TO GROW IN THIS AREA.**

**4: HOW WAS YOUR PATIENCE TODAY, WHY WAS THIS? WHAT
COULD YOU DO DIFFERENTLY TOMORROW?**

**5: DID YOU DO ANY MENTORING TODAY, WHY WAS THIS? HOW
COULD YOU DEVELOP THIS AREA?**

6: HOW MUCH ACTIVE LISTENING DID YOU DO TODAY? DID YOU ACTUALLY LISTEN TO UNDERSTAND OR LISTEN TO REPLY? HOW COULD YOU IMPROVE ON THIS AREA FOR TOMORROW?

7: HOW WERE YOUR COMMUNICATION SKILLS TODAY? HOW COULD YOU IMPROVE IN THIS AREA? LITTLE CHANGES TO REALLY UNDERSTAND THE HUGE AREA OF COMMUNICATION WITH DIFFERENT PERSONALITIES.

8: HOW DEPENDABLE DO YOU THINK YOU WERE TODAY? WHY WAS THIS?

9: DID YOU FIND YOURSELF PROCRASTINATING TODAY? HOW COULD YOU CHANGE THIS INTO ACTION?

DATE:-   /   /

1: HOW WAS YOUR DECISION MAKING TODAY, WHY WAS THIS? WHAT CHANGE COULD YOU MAKE TO MOVE FORWARD INTO TOMORROW?

2: WRITE ONE PROBLEM YOU SOLVED TODAY? HOW DID YOU DEAL WITH THIS? WHAT COULD YOU DO DIFFERENTLY TO IMPROVE?

3: HOW MUCH EMPATHY HAVE YOU SHOWN TODAY, WHY WAS THIS? HOW DID YOU FEEL DEALING WITH EMPATHY? THINK ABOUT A CHANGE TO GROW IN THIS AREA.

4: HOW WAS YOUR PATIENCE TODAY, WHY WAS THIS? WHAT COULD YOU DO DIFFERENTLY TOMORROW?

5: DID YOU DO ANY MENTORING TODAY, WHY WAS THIS? HOW COULD YOU DEVELOP THIS AREA?

6: HOW MUCH ACTIVE LISTENING DID YOU DO TODAY? DID YOU ACTUALLY LISTEN TO UNDERSTAND OR LISTEN TO REPLY? HOW COULD YOU IMPROVE ON THIS AREA FOR TOMORROW?

7: HOW WERE YOUR COMMUNICATION SKILLS TODAY? HOW COULD YOU IMPROVE IN THIS AREA? LITTLE CHANGES TO REALLY UNDERSTAND THE HUGE AREA OF COMMUNICATION WITH DIFFERENT PERSONALITIES.

8: HOW DEPENDABLE DO YOU THINK YOU WERE TODAY? WHY WAS THIS?

9: DID YOU FIND YOURSELF PROCRASTINATING TODAY? HOW COULD YOU CHANGE THIS INTO ACTION?

DATE:-   /   /

1: HOW WAS YOUR DECISION MAKING TODAY, WHY WAS THIS?
WHAT CHANGE COULD YOU MAKE TO MOVE FORWARD INTO TOMORROW?

2: WRITE ONE PROBLEM YOU SOLVED TODAY? HOW DID YOU DEAL
WITH THIS? WHAT COULD YOU DO DIFFERENTLY TO IMPROVE?

3: HOW MUCH EMPATHY HAVE YOU SHOWN TODAY, WHY WAS THIS?
HOW DID YOU FEEL DEALING WITH EMPATHY? THINK ABOUT A CHANGE
TO GROW IN THIS AREA.

4: HOW WAS YOUR PATIENCE TODAY, WHY WAS THIS? WHAT
COULD YOU DO DIFFERENTLY TOMORROW?

5: DID YOU DO ANY MENTORING TODAY, WHY WAS THIS? HOW
COULD YOU DEVELOP THIS AREA?

6: HOW MUCH ACTIVE LISTENING DID YOU DO TODAY? DID YOU ACTUALLY LISTEN TO UNDERSTAND OR LISTEN TO REPLY? HOW COULD YOU IMPROVE ON THIS AREA FOR TOMORROW?

7: HOW WERE YOUR COMMUNICATION SKILLS TODAY? HOW COULD YOU IMPROVE IN THIS AREA? LITTLE CHANGES TO REALLY UNDERSTAND THE HUGE AREA OF COMMUNICATION WITH DIFFERENT PERSONALITIES.

8: HOW DEPENDABLE DO YOU THINK YOU WERE TODAY? WHY WAS THIS?

9: DID YOU FIND YOURSELF PROCRASTINATING TODAY? HOW COULD YOU CHANGE THIS INTO ACTION?

DATE:-   /   /

1: HOW WAS YOUR DECISION MAKING TODAY, WHY WAS THIS?
WHAT CHANGE COULD YOU MAKE TO MOVE FORWARD INTO TOMORROW?

2: WRITE ONE PROBLEM YOU SOLVED TODAY? HOW DID YOU DEAL
WITH THIS? WHAT COULD YOU DO DIFFERENTLY TO IMPROVE?

3: HOW MUCH EMPATHY HAVE YOU SHOWN TODAY, WHY WAS THIS?
HOW DID YOU FEEL DEALING WITH EMPATHY? THINK ABOUT A CHANGE
TO GROW IN THIS AREA.

4: HOW WAS YOUR PATIENCE TODAY, WHY WAS THIS? WHAT
COULD YOU DO DIFFERENTLY TOMORROW?

5: DID YOU DO ANY MENTORING TODAY, WHY WAS THIS? HOW
COULD YOU DEVELOP THIS AREA?

6: HOW MUCH ACTIVE LISTENING DID YOU DO TODAY? DID YOU ACTUALLY LISTEN TO UNDERSTAND OR LISTEN TO REPLY? HOW COULD YOU IMPROVE ON THIS AREA FOR TOMORROW?

7: HOW WERE YOUR COMMUNICATION SKILLS TODAY? HOW COULD YOU IMPROVE IN THIS AREA? LITTLE CHANGES TO REALLY UNDERSTAND THE HUGE AREA OF COMMUNICATION WITH DIFFERENT PERSONALITIES.

8: HOW DEPENDABLE DO YOU THINK YOU WERE TODAY? WHY WAS THIS?

9: DID YOU FIND YOURSELF PROCRASTINATING TODAY? HOW COULD YOU CHANGE THIS INTO ACTION?

DATE:-   /   /

1: HOW WAS YOUR DECISION MAKING TODAY, WHY WAS THIS?
WHAT CHANGE COULD YOU MAKE TO MOVE FORWARD INTO TOMORROW?

2: WRITE ONE PROBLEM YOU SOLVED TODAY? HOW DID YOU DEAL
WITH THIS? WHAT COULD YOU DO DIFFERENTLY TO IMPROVE?

3: HOW MUCH EMPATHY HAVE YOU SHOWN TODAY, WHY WAS THIS?
HOW DID YOU FEEL DEALING WITH EMPATHY? THINK ABOUT A CHANGE
TO GROW IN THIS AREA.

4: HOW WAS YOUR PATIENCE TODAY, WHY WAS THIS? WHAT
COULD YOU DO DIFFERENTLY TOMORROW?

5: DID YOU DO ANY MENTORING TODAY, WHY WAS THIS? HOW
COULD YOU DEVELOP THIS AREA?

6: HOW MUCH ACTIVE LISTENING DID YOU DO TODAY? DID YOU ACTUALLY LISTEN TO UNDERSTAND OR LISTEN TO REPLY? HOW COULD YOU IMPROVE ON THIS AREA FOR TOMORROW?

7: HOW WERE YOUR COMMUNICATION SKILLS TODAY? HOW COULD YOU IMPROVE IN THIS AREA? LITTLE CHANGES TO REALLY UNDERSTAND THE HUGE AREA OF COMMUNICATION WITH DIFFERENT PERSONALITIES.

8: HOW DEPENDABLE DO YOU THINK YOU WERE TODAY? WHY WAS THIS?

9: DID YOU FIND YOURSELF PROCRASTINATING TODAY? HOW COULD YOU CHANGE THIS INTO ACTION?

DATE:-   /   /

1: HOW WAS YOUR DECISION MAKING TODAY, WHY WAS THIS? WHAT CHANGE COULD YOU MAKE TO MOVE FORWARD INTO TOMORROW?

2: WRITE ONE PROBLEM YOU SOLVED TODAY? HOW DID YOU DEAL WITH THIS? WHAT COULD YOU DO DIFFERENTLY TO IMPROVE?

3: HOW MUCH EMPATHY HAVE YOU SHOWN TODAY, WHY WAS THIS? HOW DID YOU FEEL DEALING WITH EMPATHY? THINK ABOUT A CHANGE TO GROW IN THIS AREA.

4: HOW WAS YOUR PATIENCE TODAY, WHY WAS THIS? WHAT COULD YOU DO DIFFERENTLY TOMORROW?

5: DID YOU DO ANY MENTORING TODAY, WHY WAS THIS? HOW COULD YOU DEVELOP THIS AREA?

6: HOW MUCH ACTIVE LISTENING DID YOU DO TODAY? DID YOU ACTUALLY LISTEN TO UNDERSTAND OR LISTEN TO REPLY? HOW COULD YOU IMPROVE ON THIS AREA FOR TOMORROW?

7: HOW WERE YOUR COMMUNICATION SKILLS TODAY? HOW COULD YOU IMPROVE IN THIS AREA? LITTLE CHANGES TO REALLY UNDERSTAND THE HUGE AREA OF COMMUNICATION WITH DIFFERENT PERSONALITIES.

8: HOW DEPENDABLE DO YOU THINK YOU WERE TODAY? WHY WAS THIS?

9: DID YOU FIND YOURSELF PROCRASTINATING TODAY? HOW COULD YOU CHANGE THIS INTO ACTION?

1: HOW HAVE I GROWN OVER THE LAST 10 DAYS

2: WHAT AM I GOING TO FOCUS ON OVER THE NEXT 10 DAYS?

3: WHAT FIVE THINGS AM I POSITIVELY TAKING FROM THE LAST 10 DAYS AND MOVING THEM FORWARD INTO THE NEXT 10 DAYS.

-
-
-
-
-

4: WHAT KEY AREAS WOULD I LIKE TO CONCENTRATE ON?

"Leaders don't blame they accept responsibility."

CLAIRE MOODY

DATE:-   /   /

1: HOW WAS YOUR DECISION MAKING TODAY, WHY WAS THIS? WHAT CHANGE COULD YOU MAKE TO MOVE FORWARD INTO TOMORROW?

2: WRITE ONE PROBLEM YOU SOLVED TODAY? HOW DID YOU DEAL WITH THIS? WHAT COULD YOU DO DIFFERENTLY TO IMPROVE?

3: HOW MUCH EMPATHY HAVE YOU SHOWN TODAY, WHY WAS THIS? HOW DID YOU FEEL DEALING WITH EMPATHY? THINK ABOUT A CHANGE TO GROW IN THIS AREA.

4: HOW WAS YOUR PATIENCE TODAY, WHY WAS THIS? WHAT COULD YOU DO DIFFERENTLY TOMORROW?

5: DID YOU DO ANY MENTORING TODAY, WHY WAS THIS? HOW COULD YOU DEVELOP THIS AREA?

6: HOW MUCH ACTIVE LISTENING DID YOU DO TODAY? DID YOU ACTUALLY LISTEN TO UNDERSTAND OR LISTEN TO REPLY? HOW COULD YOU IMPROVE ON THIS AREA FOR TOMORROW?

7: HOW WERE YOUR COMMUNICATION SKILLS TODAY? HOW COULD YOU IMPROVE IN THIS AREA? LITTLE CHANGES TO REALLY UNDERSTAND THE HUGE AREA OF COMMUNICATION WITH DIFFERENT PERSONALITIES.

8: HOW DEPENDABLE DO YOU THINK YOU WERE TODAY? WHY WAS THIS?

9: DID YOU FIND YOURSELF PROCRASTINATING TODAY? HOW COULD YOU CHANGE THIS INTO ACTION?

DATE:-   /   /

1: HOW WAS YOUR DECISION MAKING TODAY, WHY WAS THIS?
WHAT CHANGE COULD YOU MAKE TO MOVE FORWARD INTO TOMORROW?

2: WRITE ONE PROBLEM YOU SOLVED TODAY? HOW DID YOU DEAL
WITH THIS? WHAT COULD YOU DO DIFFERENTLY TO IMPROVE?

3: HOW MUCH EMPATHY HAVE YOU SHOWN TODAY, WHY WAS THIS?
HOW DID YOU FEEL DEALING WITH EMPATHY? THINK ABOUT A CHANGE
TO GROW IN THIS AREA.

4: HOW WAS YOUR PATIENCE TODAY, WHY WAS THIS? WHAT
COULD YOU DO DIFFERENTLY TOMORROW?

5: DID YOU DO ANY MENTORING TODAY, WHY WAS THIS? HOW
COULD YOU DEVELOP THIS AREA?

6: HOW MUCH ACTIVE LISTENING DID YOU DO TODAY? DID YOU ACTUALLY LISTEN TO UNDERSTAND OR LISTEN TO REPLY? HOW COULD YOU IMPROVE ON THIS AREA FOR TOMORROW?

7: HOW WERE YOUR COMMUNICATION SKILLS TODAY? HOW COULD YOU IMPROVE IN THIS AREA? LITTLE CHANGES TO REALLY UNDERSTAND THE HUGE AREA OF COMMUNICATION WITH DIFFERENT PERSONALITIES.

8: HOW DEPENDABLE DO YOU THINK YOU WERE TODAY? WHY WAS THIS?

9: DID YOU FIND YOURSELF PROCRASTINATING TODAY? HOW COULD YOU CHANGE THIS INTO ACTION?

DATE:-   /   /

1: HOW WAS YOUR DECISION MAKING TODAY, WHY WAS THIS?
WHAT CHANGE COULD YOU MAKE TO MOVE FORWARD INTO TOMORROW?

2: WRITE ONE PROBLEM YOU SOLVED TODAY? HOW DID YOU DEAL
WITH THIS? WHAT COULD YOU DO DIFFERENTLY TO IMPROVE?

3: HOW MUCH EMPATHY HAVE YOU SHOWN TODAY, WHY WAS THIS?
HOW DID YOU FEEL DEALING WITH EMPATHY? THINK ABOUT A CHANGE
TO GROW IN THIS AREA.

4: HOW WAS YOUR PATIENCE TODAY, WHY WAS THIS? WHAT
COULD YOU DO DIFFERENTLY TOMORROW?

5: DID YOU DO ANY MENTORING TODAY, WHY WAS THIS? HOW
COULD YOU DEVELOP THIS AREA?

6: HOW MUCH ACTIVE LISTENING DID YOU DO TODAY? DID YOU ACTUALLY LISTEN TO UNDERSTAND OR LISTEN TO REPLY? HOW COULD YOU IMPROVE ON THIS AREA FOR TOMORROW?

7: HOW WERE YOUR COMMUNICATION SKILLS TODAY? HOW COULD YOU IMPROVE IN THIS AREA? LITTLE CHANGES TO REALLY UNDERSTAND THE HUGE AREA OF COMMUNICATION WITH DIFFERENT PERSONALITIES.

8: HOW DEPENDABLE DO YOU THINK YOU WERE TODAY? WHY WAS THIS?

9: DID YOU FIND YOURSELF PROCRASTINATING TODAY? HOW COULD YOU CHANGE THIS INTO ACTION?

DATE:-   /   /

1: HOW WAS YOUR DECISION MAKING TODAY, WHY WAS THIS? WHAT CHANGE COULD YOU MAKE TO MOVE FORWARD INTO TOMORROW?

2: WRITE ONE PROBLEM YOU SOLVED TODAY? HOW DID YOU DEAL WITH THIS? WHAT COULD YOU DO DIFFERENTLY TO IMPROVE?

3: HOW MUCH EMPATHY HAVE YOU SHOWN TODAY, WHY WAS THIS? HOW DID YOU FEEL DEALING WITH EMPATHY? THINK ABOUT A CHANGE TO GROW IN THIS AREA.

4: HOW WAS YOUR PATIENCE TODAY, WHY WAS THIS? WHAT COULD YOU DO DIFFERENTLY TOMORROW?

5: DID YOU DO ANY MENTORING TODAY, WHY WAS THIS? HOW COULD YOU DEVELOP THIS AREA?

6: HOW MUCH ACTIVE LISTENING DID YOU DO TODAY? DID YOU ACTUALLY LISTEN TO UNDERSTAND OR LISTEN TO REPLY? HOW COULD YOU IMPROVE ON THIS AREA FOR TOMORROW?

7: HOW WERE YOUR COMMUNICATION SKILLS TODAY? HOW COULD YOU IMPROVE IN THIS AREA? LITTLE CHANGES TO REALLY UNDERSTAND THE HUGE AREA OF COMMUNICATION WITH DIFFERENT PERSONALITIES.

8: HOW DEPENDABLE DO YOU THINK YOU WERE TODAY? WHY WAS THIS?

9: DID YOU FIND YOURSELF PROCRASTINATING TODAY? HOW COULD YOU CHANGE THIS INTO ACTION?

DATE:-   /   /

1: HOW WAS YOUR DECISION MAKING TODAY, WHY WAS THIS?
WHAT CHANGE COULD YOU MAKE TO MOVE FORWARD INTO TOMORROW?

2: WRITE ONE PROBLEM YOU SOLVED TODAY? HOW DID YOU DEAL
WITH THIS? WHAT COULD YOU DO DIFFERENTLY TO IMPROVE?

3: HOW MUCH EMPATHY HAVE YOU SHOWN TODAY, WHY WAS THIS?
HOW DID YOU FEEL DEALING WITH EMPATHY? THINK ABOUT A CHANGE
TO GROW IN THIS AREA.

4: HOW WAS YOUR PATIENCE TODAY, WHY WAS THIS? WHAT
COULD YOU DO DIFFERENTLY TOMORROW?

5: DID YOU DO ANY MENTORING TODAY, WHY WAS THIS? HOW
COULD YOU DEVELOP THIS AREA?

6: HOW MUCH ACTIVE LISTENING DID YOU DO TODAY? DID YOU ACTUALLY LISTEN TO UNDERSTAND OR LISTEN TO REPLY? HOW COULD YOU IMPROVE ON THIS AREA FOR TOMORROW?

7: HOW WERE YOUR COMMUNICATION SKILLS TODAY? HOW COULD YOU IMPROVE IN THIS AREA? LITTLE CHANGES TO REALLY UNDERSTAND THE HUGE AREA OF COMMUNICATION WITH DIFFERENT PERSONALITIES.

8: HOW DEPENDABLE DO YOU THINK YOU WERE TODAY? WHY WAS THIS?

9: DID YOU FIND YOURSELF PROCRASTINATING TODAY? HOW COULD YOU CHANGE THIS INTO ACTION?

EFFECTIVE LEADER JOURNAL

DATE:-   /   /

1: HOW WAS YOUR DECISION MAKING TODAY, WHY WAS THIS? WHAT CHANGE COULD YOU MAKE TO MOVE FORWARD INTO TOMORROW?

2: WRITE ONE PROBLEM YOU SOLVED TODAY? HOW DID YOU DEAL WITH THIS? WHAT COULD YOU DO DIFFERENTLY TO IMPROVE?

3: HOW MUCH EMPATHY HAVE YOU SHOWN TODAY, WHY WAS THIS? HOW DID YOU FEEL DEALING WITH EMPATHY? THINK ABOUT A CHANGE TO GROW IN THIS AREA.

4: HOW WAS YOUR PATIENCE TODAY, WHY WAS THIS? WHAT COULD YOU DO DIFFERENTLY TOMORROW?

5: DID YOU DO ANY MENTORING TODAY, WHY WAS THIS? HOW COULD YOU DEVELOP THIS AREA?

6: HOW MUCH ACTIVE LISTENING DID YOU DO TODAY? DID YOU ACTUALLY LISTEN TO UNDERSTAND OR LISTEN TO REPLY? HOW COULD YOU IMPROVE ON THIS AREA FOR TOMORROW?

7: HOW WERE YOUR COMMUNICATION SKILLS TODAY? HOW COULD YOU IMPROVE IN THIS AREA? LITTLE CHANGES TO REALLY UNDERSTAND THE HUGE AREA OF COMMUNICATION WITH DIFFERENT PERSONALITIES.

8: HOW DEPENDABLE DO YOU THINK YOU WERE TODAY? WHY WAS THIS?

9: DID YOU FIND YOURSELF PROCRASTINATING TODAY? HOW COULD YOU CHANGE THIS INTO ACTION?

DATE:-   /   /

1: HOW WAS YOUR DECISION MAKING TODAY, WHY WAS THIS? WHAT CHANGE COULD YOU MAKE TO MOVE FORWARD INTO TOMORROW?

2: WRITE ONE PROBLEM YOU SOLVED TODAY? HOW DID YOU DEAL WITH THIS? WHAT COULD YOU DO DIFFERENTLY TO IMPROVE?

3: HOW MUCH EMPATHY HAVE YOU SHOWN TODAY, WHY WAS THIS? HOW DID YOU FEEL DEALING WITH EMPATHY? THINK ABOUT A CHANGE TO GROW IN THIS AREA.

4: HOW WAS YOUR PATIENCE TODAY, WHY WAS THIS? WHAT COULD YOU DO DIFFERENTLY TOMORROW?

5: DID YOU DO ANY MENTORING TODAY, WHY WAS THIS? HOW COULD YOU DEVELOP THIS AREA?

6: HOW MUCH ACTIVE LISTENING DID YOU DO TODAY? DID YOU ACTUALLY LISTEN TO UNDERSTAND OR LISTEN TO REPLY? HOW COULD YOU IMPROVE ON THIS AREA FOR TOMORROW?

7: HOW WERE YOUR COMMUNICATION SKILLS TODAY? HOW COULD YOU IMPROVE IN THIS AREA? LITTLE CHANGES TO REALLY UNDERSTAND THE HUGE AREA OF COMMUNICATION WITH DIFFERENT PERSONALITIES.

8: HOW DEPENDABLE DO YOU THINK YOU WERE TODAY? WHY WAS THIS?

9: DID YOU FIND YOURSELF PROCRASTINATING TODAY? HOW COULD YOU CHANGE THIS INTO ACTION?

DATE:-   /   /

1: HOW WAS YOUR DECISION MAKING TODAY, WHY WAS THIS? WHAT CHANGE COULD YOU MAKE TO MOVE FORWARD INTO TOMORROW?

2: WRITE ONE PROBLEM YOU SOLVED TODAY? HOW DID YOU DEAL WITH THIS? WHAT COULD YOU DO DIFFERENTLY TO IMPROVE?

3: HOW MUCH EMPATHY HAVE YOU SHOWN TODAY, WHY WAS THIS? HOW DID YOU FEEL DEALING WITH EMPATHY? THINK ABOUT A CHANGE TO GROW IN THIS AREA.

4: HOW WAS YOUR PATIENCE TODAY, WHY WAS THIS? WHAT COULD YOU DO DIFFERENTLY TOMORROW?

5: DID YOU DO ANY MENTORING TODAY, WHY WAS THIS? HOW COULD YOU DEVELOP THIS AREA?

6: HOW MUCH ACTIVE LISTENING DID YOU DO TODAY? DID YOU ACTUALLY LISTEN TO UNDERSTAND OR LISTEN TO REPLY? HOW COULD YOU IMPROVE ON THIS AREA FOR TOMORROW?

7: HOW WERE YOUR COMMUNICATION SKILLS TODAY? HOW COULD YOU IMPROVE IN THIS AREA? LITTLE CHANGES TO REALLY UNDERSTAND THE HUGE AREA OF COMMUNICATION WITH DIFFERENT PERSONALITIES.

8: HOW DEPENDABLE DO YOU THINK YOU WERE TODAY? WHY WAS THIS?

9: DID YOU FIND YOURSELF PROCRASTINATING TODAY? HOW COULD YOU CHANGE THIS INTO ACTION?

EFFECTIVE LEADER JOURNAL

DATE:-   /   /

1: HOW WAS YOUR DECISION MAKING TODAY, WHY WAS THIS? WHAT CHANGE COULD YOU MAKE TO MOVE FORWARD INTO TOMORROW?

2: WRITE ONE PROBLEM YOU SOLVED TODAY? HOW DID YOU DEAL WITH THIS? WHAT COULD YOU DO DIFFERENTLY TO IMPROVE?

3: HOW MUCH EMPATHY HAVE YOU SHOWN TODAY, WHY WAS THIS? HOW DID YOU FEEL DEALING WITH EMPATHY? THINK ABOUT A CHANGE TO GROW IN THIS AREA.

4: HOW WAS YOUR PATIENCE TODAY, WHY WAS THIS? WHAT COULD YOU DO DIFFERENTLY TOMORROW?

5: DID YOU DO ANY MENTORING TODAY, WHY WAS THIS? HOW COULD YOU DEVELOP THIS AREA?

6: HOW MUCH ACTIVE LISTENING DID YOU DO TODAY? DID YOU ACTUALLY LISTEN TO UNDERSTAND OR LISTEN TO REPLY? HOW COULD YOU IMPROVE ON THIS AREA FOR TOMORROW?

7: HOW WERE YOUR COMMUNICATION SKILLS TODAY? HOW COULD YOU IMPROVE IN THIS AREA? LITTLE CHANGES TO REALLY UNDERSTAND THE HUGE AREA OF COMMUNICATION WITH DIFFERENT PERSONALITIES.

8: HOW DEPENDABLE DO YOU THINK YOU WERE TODAY? WHY WAS THIS?

9: DID YOU FIND YOURSELF PROCRASTINATING TODAY? HOW COULD YOU CHANGE THIS INTO ACTION?

DATE:-   /   /

1: HOW WAS YOUR DECISION MAKING TODAY, WHY WAS THIS? WHAT CHANGE COULD YOU MAKE TO MOVE FORWARD INTO TOMORROW?

2: WRITE ONE PROBLEM YOU SOLVED TODAY? HOW DID YOU DEAL WITH THIS? WHAT COULD YOU DO DIFFERENTLY TO IMPROVE?

3: HOW MUCH EMPATHY HAVE YOU SHOWN TODAY, WHY WAS THIS? HOW DID YOU FEEL DEALING WITH EMPATHY? THINK ABOUT A CHANGE TO GROW IN THIS AREA.

4: HOW WAS YOUR PATIENCE TODAY, WHY WAS THIS? WHAT COULD YOU DO DIFFERENTLY TOMORROW?

5: DID YOU DO ANY MENTORING TODAY, WHY WAS THIS? HOW COULD YOU DEVELOP THIS AREA?

6: HOW MUCH ACTIVE LISTENING DID YOU DO TODAY? DID YOU ACTUALLY LISTEN TO UNDERSTAND OR LISTEN TO REPLY? HOW COULD YOU IMPROVE ON THIS AREA FOR TOMORROW?

7: HOW WERE YOUR COMMUNICATION SKILLS TODAY? HOW COULD YOU IMPROVE IN THIS AREA? LITTLE CHANGES TO REALLY UNDERSTAND THE HUGE AREA OF COMMUNICATION WITH DIFFERENT PERSONALITIES.

8: HOW DEPENDABLE DO YOU THINK YOU WERE TODAY? WHY WAS THIS?

9: DID YOU FIND YOURSELF PROCRASTINATING TODAY? HOW COULD YOU CHANGE THIS INTO ACTION?

1: HOW HAVE I GROWN OVER THE LAST 10 DAYS

2: WHAT AM I GOING TO FOCUS ON OVER THE NEXT 10 DAYS?

3: WHAT FIVE THINGS AM I POSITIVELY TAKING FROM THE LAST 10 DAYS AND MOVING THEM FORWARD INTO THE NEXT 10 DAYS.

-
-
-
-
-

4: WHAT KEY AREAS WOULD I LIKE TO CONCENTRATE ON?

Day 100
Congratulations

Congratulations on achieving 100 days. You have completed and reflected on being an effective leader. You have created some very positive actions. You have our permission to give yourself an award for achieving this fantastic milestone. Now think about how you can take this forward and grow further, amazing stuff.

WHAT HAVE I LEARNT AND HOW AM I GOING TO IMPLEMENT THIS IN THE FUTURE

WRITE FIVE THINGS THAT YOU HAVE BECOME MUCH MORE AWARE OF. THE JOURNAL HAS GIVEN YOU LITTLE SPACES TO WRITE KEY THINGS DOWN, OBVIOUSLY THE GREATER THE REFLECTION THE MORE YOU IMPROVE. THE PROBLEM IS NOT EVERYONE IS AWARE WRITING DOWN WORKS, THIS JOURNAL KEEPS IT EASY FOR YOU.

GOOD LUCK WITH MOVING FORWARD, BE PROUD OF YOURSELF.

1..

2..

3..

4..

5..

If you have enjoyed this journal please leave us a review on Amazon.

NOTES

JCRM JOURNALS
MEET THE AUTHORS

www.jcrmjournals.com

RALPH MOODY

Ralph believes that lifelong learning is precisely that, and should not be limited by age or perceived ability. He has a belief that all of us have the potential to do anything if we put our minds to it. Armed with the right skills, knowledge and attitude, we can all perform to the highest standards. Moreover, his philosophy is that limiting belief is what holds the majority of people back and that, with appropriate coaching, mentoring and training, we can all achieve anything. With over 30 years of training experience, he specialises in trainer, management and leadership development.

> *"Life is a gift and we all have a responsibility to make the most of it, so that when we look back, we know it wasn't wasted"*
>
> RALPH MOODY

CLAIRE MOODY

Claire is an extremely experienced trainer and coach at Target Training, and you can always guarantee she will deliver outstanding results: she is incredibly passionate about both her training and coaching. She has over 35 years' experience in training, coaching and quality assurance roles, with experience as a teacher and in Train the Trainer, working with international clients. Moreover, she has expertise in the management of trainer inductions, standardisation and quality assurance for corporate clients. She holds an MSc in executive coaching and is accredited by Ashridge, a world leader in executive coach training and development. Additionally, she specialises in psychometric assessment, including MBTI.

> *"It's not about being the best, it's about being the best you can be"*
>
> CLAIRE MOODY

HAVE QUESTIONS?

Target Training Associates
107 Cheapside, London, EC2V 6DN
0800 302 9344
info@targettrg.co.uk
www.targettrg.co.uk
www.jcrmjournals.com

SOME OTHER TITLES IN THE JOURNAL SERIES

Coaching Journal
Training Journal
Being Positive Journal
Improve Self-Esteem Journal
Do I or don't I deal with conflict Journal
Action Planning Journal
Management Journal
Rainbow Foods Journal

Contact us for a quote for a bespoke journal for your particular organisation

www.ingramcontent.com/pod-product-compliance
Lightning Source LLC
Chambersburg PA
CBHW021358210526
45463CB00001B/148